Saudi Arabian Oil Policy and the Iran-Iraq War

What Drives Saudi Arabian Oil Policy?

Alexander John Hay

Copyright and Disclaimers

Saudi Arabian Oil Policy and the Iran-Iraq War
By Alexander John Hay

Originally produced in 1987 in partial fulfillment of the requirements for the degree with honors of Bachelor of Arts for the Department of Government, Harvard College. Changes have been made to the Introduction, and typographical errors corrected.

Copyright 2015 - 2023, Alexander John Hay
All Rights Reserved

No Portion of this publication may be reproduced or transmitted in any form or by any means, electronic or mechanical, including, but not limited to, audio recordings, facsimiles, photocopying, or information storage and retrieval systems without explicit written permission from the author or publisher.

Published By:

Alexander John Hay
364 East Main Street, Suite 215
Middletown, DE 19709
www.Alexander-Hay.com

Legal Disclaimer:

The author and publisher reserve the right to make any changes they deem necessary to future versions of the publication to ensure its accuracy.

The reader assumes all responsibility for the use of the information within this report.

Table of Contents

Preface..1
Chapter 1: Introduction.......................................6
Chapter 2: Oil Price Theory................................14
    Overview..14
    The Dominant Producer and Economic self-interest 14
    OPEC Decision Making..................................17
    Economic Modeling.......................................18
    The Political Model.......................................22
Chapter 3: The 1970s..26
    Overview..26
    The 1973 Oil Embargo and aftermath............27
    Moderation between 1974 to 1979................31
    1978 and the Price Increases of 1979............33
    Summer 1979 to the Iran-Iraq War...............38
Chapter 4: The Iran-Iraq War – September 1980 to March 1982..43
    Overview..43
    The Swing Producer as OPEC Leader.............44
    Threats and Opportunities for Saudi Arabia...48
    The Stalemate and Saudi Arabian Oil Policy through 1981..50
    The Islamic Conference and Iranian Resistance.......51
    The Iranian Offensives of 1981-1982.............54
    The Iraqi Withdrawal....................................60
    The Aftermath...62

Chapter 5: Saudi Arabian Oil Policy – Summer of 1982 to 1985..64
    Overview..64
    The Role of the Radicals and Saudi Arabia..............65
    The Gulf and the Iran-Iraq War from March 1982 to January 1983...67
    The Invasion of Iraq..71
    Saudi Arabian Oil Policy from 1983 to 1985............73
    The London Agreement...74
    The Renewed Stalemate 1983...................................76
    The Gulf Dimension 1984...79
    The 1985 Deterioration of OPEC..............................83

Chapter 6: The Price War – August 1985 to December 1986..84
    Overview..84
    The End of the Swing Producer................................84
    The Price War...88
    The Gulf War..90
    1986 to the End of the Price War.............................93
    The End of the Price War...94
    The December OPEC Agreement.............................99

Chapter 7: Conclusion...103
    The Noble Oil..103

Post Script..107

BIBLIOGRAPHY...109
    Journals and Annuals..112

About the Author..113

Saudi Arabian Oil Policy and the Iran-Iraq War

Preface

This book is based wholly upon my senior thesis which was presented to the Government Department of Harvard College in the Spring of 1987. The title of my thesis was <u>Saudi Arabian Oil Policy: Its Political Implications</u>. I began research on the subject in 1985 during my sophomore year of college, and was lucky enough to have Laurie Mylroie as my faculty advisor after being directed to her by Nadav Safran.

Much to the surprise of my advisor I completed the thesis on time and successfully submitted it for consideration to the Government Department. It was received with some approval and I was able to graduate with honors. I say "surprise" because I did not start working on the final draft until January of 1987, the last semester of my senior year, and it was due in March of 1987. Ordinarily you are supposed to have your final draft done in the last semester of your junior year so that you can spend your senior year in a leisurely process of review and finalization.

Unfortunately I did not have that luxury. Laurie Mylroie believed that the reason for my delay in getting started on the final draft was based upon my penchant for procrastination. There is clearly some truth in this. However, the real problem rested with the subject matter of my thesis: The Iran-Iraq War.

The Iran-Iraq War began in September of 1980 and continued on until August of 1988. I was writing about an ongoing conflict that was in constant flux right up to December of 1986. In fact 1986 proved to be a pivotal year in the war, and of tremendous importance in regards to the premise of my thesis. So instead of settling down and producing a rough draft prior to my senior year,

Saudi Arabian Oil Policy and the Iran-Iraq War

I was busy continuing with my research up to December of 1986, the first semester of my senior year.

When I came back from Christmas break and met with Laurie Mylroie about my progress she was extremely displeased with me. She pointed out that she had never heard of a student successfully completing their thesis without having a final draft in the hands of their advisor by the end of the first semester of the senior year. I told her I was extremely confident in my ability to produce a final draft by mid-February based upon my unwavering confidence in my system of research which had never failed me. She was quite correctly skeptical.

My research method was based upon the old fashioned index card system. During my research whenever I found anything that seemed remotely useful, I prepared an index card containing all the bibliographic information about the source, and an index card containing each individual item of information from that source. By January of 1987 I had several shoe boxes full of index cards containing all the research I had done during the prior two years, and a rather detailed outline of the proposed thesis. All I had to do was organize the cards under the various headings of my outline, and then write the contents of those index cards into the outline with appropriate filler material. How difficult could that be?

Needless to say I grossly miscalculated how much time it would take me to accomplish this task. The process of organizing the cards was easy enough, but converting them into a 130 page document with complete endnotes and a bibliography turned out to be a more time consuming process than I had envisioned.

The fact that I completed my final draft by mid-February as I had promised was due primarily to copious consumption of coffee, Rothman cigarettes, and Bushmill's Irish Whiskey. With this combination of stimulants to keep me awake and whiskey to calm my jittery nerves I was able to produce a final draft that Lauri Mylroie helped me to turn into a completed thesis.

Saudi Arabian Oil Policy and the Iran-Iraq War

I look back with regret about how unfair I was to Dr. Mylroie. I was not her only student, and I presumed too much of her. She had many other responsibilities to deal with. Luckily for me she was willing to put in the long hours required to turn my rough draft into a final product. I am quite sure that most other professors would have simply told me that I had waited too long, and that I was on my own. They would have kicked me out of their office with a sneering, "Good luck kid."

In addition to her tireless efforts at proofreading my final draft, she also provided me with extremely good advice in regards to university politics. You see the subject matter of my thesis was in hot dispute among various experts in the field, and my analysis concluded that they were all wrong. Not a very wise position for an undergraduate student to take in regards to the leaders in the field, many of whom were petty, vindictive, and venal, and probable graders of my thesis. I had to walk a very fine line between proving my point, and insulting people who could cause me to not only fail to graduate with honors, but to fail to graduate at all.

The subject of my thesis was not only the Iran-Iraq War, but also Saudi Arabian Oil Policy. At the time there were three schools of thought that dominated the various factions within the Middle Eastern Studies field:

1. The Economic Rationality Model held that Saudi Arabian oil policy was defined by the model of Saudi Arabia making decisions as an economically rational actor with its long-term economic interests as the primary priority. As such Saudi Arabian oil policy could be completely analyzed and predicted using accurate economic models.

Saudi Arabian Oil Policy and the Iran-Iraq War

2. The Macro Political Model held that Saudi Arabia was more concerned with international political issues, specifically, the Cold War and opposing Soviet influence in the Middle East.

3. The Micro Political Model held that Saudi Arabia was primarily concerned with the Israeli-Palestinian conflict, and that all its policy considerations were driven by these concerns.

I took a decidedly different approach. I suggested that the overwhelming concern behind Saudi Arabian economic and political policies had little to do with economic models or the above political issues. The primary concern of the Saudi leadership was SURVIVAL.

The rulers of Saudi Arabia are a relatively small Arabian family-tribal group, the Sa'uds (roughly 3,000 to 5,000 individuals at the time). This ruling elite ruled a country of five to eight million people, many of whom had only tenuous connections with the Sa'ud family, and often little love. Surrounding Saudi Arabia were powerfully and dangerous rivals who mostly resented and envied the Sa'uds their position and wealth. The Sa'ud family ruled over a nation filled with potentially dangerous subjects which was surrounded by hostile neighbors who would like nothing more than to see their rule collapse and all of them put to the sword, while at the same time enriching themselves with the resources of Saudi Arabia.

Simply put, the rulers of Saudi Arabia did not have the luxury of committing their country to economic rationality, and most certainly could not worry a great deal about such grandiose issues as the Cold War, or such irrelevant issues as the Israeli-Palestinian conflict. They had to constantly worry about internal threats from their own subjects, and the very real external threats from neighboring countries.

The Iran-Iraq War provided the perfect opportunity to prove that Saudi Arabian oil policy was driven by regional political threats more than by any other concern.

However, as an undergraduate student I could not come forward with this theory, at least not in a confrontational manner. I had to dance around the subject in order to avoid insulting those above me who would most likely be grading my thesis. So I changed the title of my thesis to be rather vague, and I avoided as best I could suggesting that the above political models were in error. Rather I simply presented the evidence that contradicted the above models. I did not even mention the issue of the Israeli-Palestinian conflict since the topic is so controversial and emotionally divisive (even in academia). I more or less concluded that Saudi Arabian oil policy was a rather complicated thing that could not be easily pigeon-holed into any of the above models.

I weaseled out. But I graduated with honors.

And as for this little book, I doubt anyone will read it or consider it to be in any way useful. However, by completing and self-publishing it, I can now set aside a rather annoying compulsion and focus upon more mundane issues.

Alexander John Hay, February 25, 2015

Saudi Arabian Oil Policy and the Iran-Iraq War

Chapter 1: Introduction

This analysis focuses on Saudi Arabian oil policy in the context of Saudi decisions on both pricing and production. When comparing the immense financial resources that Saudi Arabia has in its oil reserves, with Saudi decisions on how this valuable resource is to be harnessed, one finds a dramatic conflict that needs to be reconciled.

Saudi Arabian oil reserves are the largest in the world. This fact takes on vital significance in light of the Saudi's financial position. Historically, Saudi Arabia has had rather limited financial needs which has allowed it to vary its production according to Saudi desires rather than by necessity. This has placed Saudi Arabia in the theoretical position of dominant producer within OPEC, with the ability to lower production to support OPEC pricing policy in weak markets, and raise production in order to punish members whose actions go against the wishes of OPEC or Saudi Arabia. As Saudi Arabia's former oil minister, Sheik Yamani, was quoted as saying:

> We can produce as much as 11 million barrels a day. This makes us a power to be reckoned with both by producing and consuming countries. To ruin the other countries of OPEC, all we have to do is produce to our full capacity; to ruin the consumer we only have to reduce our production.[1]

---

1 A. M. El-Mokadem, OPEC and the World Oil Market 1973-1983, (London: Easlords Publishing Ltd., 1984), pp. 28-29.

Saudi Arabian Oil Policy and the Iran-Iraq War

This would seem to suggest that Saudi Arabia has an economic latitude within OPEC that would permit it to dominate OPEC policies to promote those that would be more in line with Saudi long-term interests. Despite the above statement this has not proven to be the case. Instead, Saudi Arabia has often been forced to adopt positions within OPEC that are admittedly counter productive to its economic and national interests.

This analysis will focus on the period from the 1979 price increase up to the Saudi Arabian induced price collapse of late 1985 and early 1986, and the subsequent Saudi policy reversals in August 1986. During this period, Saudi Arabian oil policy has been determined by a mixture of many different interests, dominated by the regional political environment of the Middle East which during most of this period has been in turn dominated by the Iran-Iraq War.

In essence Saudi Arabia was often forced to use its oil reserves as a political tool in order to further its broader political interests, and/or defend its political security.

It has often been suggested that Saudi Arabian oil policy is purely an economic matter which can be suitably explained by the logic of economic theory. According to this theory, the price rise of oil is a function of economic factors based on decreasing supply and increasing demand. A price decrease is based on opposite economic factors which signal increased supply and/or decreased demand. This would suggest that past oil prices, and production policies, can be explained by economic models based on the economic rationality of an OPEC dominated by Saudi Arabia. This has not proven to be the case.

Saudi Arabian Oil Policy and the Iran-Iraq War

Economic modeling, which can at times accurately forecast the financial benefits and disadvantages of certain actions, provides neither a valid nor a complete explanation of Saudi Arabian oil policy. This is because it fails to take into account the regional power structure which Saudi Arabia, a very weak player, operates within as the major factor in deciding Saudi Arabian oil policy. This analysis offers an alternative to economic modeling which will be explained further in Chapter 1.

It is clear that for a country like Saudi Arabia with large oil deposits and relatively low financial demands the ideal long-term price for oil based on models of economic rationality would suggest keeping the price low in order to discourage conservation or replacement of oil by consumers.

Saudi Arabia has often been forced to take actions concerning oil policy which have been decidedly against its long term economic interests, and furthermore, against its long-term political interests as well. The three main examples of this phenomena are the Saudi policy reversals of 1979, 1982, and 1986. Theodore Moran demonstrated that in the 1970s, the Saudi's oil policy was economically perverse in that the Saudis failed to follow the economically rational approach of managing their resources on a long-term basis by a moderate oil policy.[2]

This does not mean that the Saudis ignored economics. Rather it suggests that in the face of more important political and security circumstances, the Saudis were willing to compromise their economic interests. In other words, the Saudis tried to follow their economic interests when they felt secure, but were quick to abandon them in the face of

---

2   Theodore H. Moran, "Modeling OPEC Behavior: Economic and Political Alternatives." International Organization, Spring 1981, passim.

conflict, or when the political situation demanded a different posture.

In the 1970s, Saudi oil policy experienced many changes, the first of which occurred in 1973. The 1973 oil embargo marks the first time that Saudi Arabia used its oil as a political tool, or weapon. It did so unwillingly and with much deliberation, but when the situation in the October War seemed to threaten vital Saudi political interests, the oil weapon was unleashed. In the case of the price increases of 1979, caused by Saudi production cuts, Saudi Arabia reversed its previous policy due to a drastic change in the regional balance of power. Whereas in 1973, Saudi participation in the Embargo served the political interests of Saudi Arabia, the 1979 Saudi price reductions were neither in its long-term economic nor its political interests, but represent Saudi Arabian reaction to short-term political pressure.

In the subsequent changes in Saudi oil policies in 1982 and in 1986, certain patterns developed: Saudi Arabia followed an economically rational policy when it felt relatively secure, and Saudi Arabia abandoned its economic interests in favor of a policy of appeasement when it felt threatened. I suggest that this change of policy away from economic rationality occurred due to short-term political pressures which Saudi Arabia was unable, or unwilling, to deal with.

Chapter 3 will give the historical background of the 1970s, showing the differences between the 1973 Oil Embargo and the 1979 price increases.

Chapter 4 will illustrate Saudi Arabian oil policy during the initial phases of the Iran-Iraq War. Phase one was an Iraqi dominated stalemate which allowed Saudi Arabia relative freedom of action; economic and political. Phase two was the

Saudi Arabian Oil Policy and the Iran-Iraq War

Iranian offensives of 1981-1982 which reversed the progress of the war in favor of Iran, and left Saudi Arabia in a politically difficult situation.

Chapter 5 will examine the period from 1982 to 1985 during which Saudi Arabia loses control of OPEC policy, and becomes the "swing producer."

Chapter 6 will appraise the Saudi led "price war" in which OPEC prices tumbled to below $10 a barrel in an effort to recapture the oil market, and the ensuing end of the price war.

The Saudi actions of early 1979 are direct examples of Saudi Arabia abandoning its economic and political long-term interests in response to a short-term danger. In this case it was a combination of the challenge that the new Islamic regime in Iran posed for Saudi Arabia and the other conservative Gulf states, and the pressure applied by the hard-line Iraqi-Syrian alliance. If they had chosen to do so, the Saudis could have kept the price of oil at reasonable levels during this period by keeping their production up, and declaring their intention of expanding production further if necessary, but this would have required a head on collision with the radicals in OPEC and in the Middle East. The Saudis chose the path of conciliation.

In late 1979 and early 1980, regional political pressures eased somewhat and there was a Saudi return to a more moderate oil policy. By July 1979, the Syrian-Iraqi alliance was breaking up, and Iraq became more moderate in an effort to win over the conservative Gulf states. In July 1979, Saudi Arabia, freed of the pressure from the Syrian-Iraqi alliance, raised its production to 9.8 million barrels per day (mbd) and kept it at this rate for more than a year. The Saudis did this in

Saudi Arabian Oil Policy and the Iran-Iraq War

the face of a fading demand for OPEC oil, and dropping spot prices.

In September 1980, the Iran-Iraq War began, and became the single most important issue in Persian Gulf and Middle Eastern politics. Within a month the war settled down into a stalemate, and Saudi Arabia raised its production to an all time high of 10.5 mbd to make up for Iraqi and Iranian production. This flooded the market and thus put great pressure on OPEC to lower the price of oil to a more moderate level. The Iran-Iraq War, in neutralizing both Iran and Iraq, gave Saudi Arabia liberty in its pursuit of its political and economic interests.

In early 1982, when Iran turned the tide of the war through a series of offensives begun in late 1981 it was only a matter of months before Saudi Arabia was forced to take on the onerous role of OPEC's "swing producer," and begin making cuts in its production in order to support the OPEC price, and allow others such as Iran. to increase its production. This was a role that was obviously not in the interest of Saudi Arabia, economically and politically. Saudi Arabia had to absorb tremendous cutbacks in production from a high of 10.5 mbd to a low of 1.9 mbd during the summer of 1985. which caused serious financial strains which Saudi Arabia has yet to resolve. Also it propped up a sagging oil market that allowed Iran to acquire revenues needed for its conflict with Iraq.

If the question of why Saudi Arabia has at different times conceded to radical demands for higher oil prices is of interest, of equal interest is why Saudi Arabia

has at different times taken the opposite approach. In late 1985, Saudi Arabia acted in open defiance of the radicals in OPEC when it began increasing its oil production above agreed levels. Many suggest that Saudi Arabia's change of production policy occurred because of the drastic financial difficulties it was facing. This is both plausible and logical, yet fails to explain an important variable: timing. If economic difficulties were the sole reason for such a change of policy, then it should have occurred much sooner. It was apparent almost immediately from its inception in 1982 that the role of the "swing producer" would be a costly one in the long-run:

> A short-term cutback... would not pose unmanageable problems in the short-term... but holding production to that level for an entire year could result in an annual Saudi deficit of $31-billion.[3]

This in fact proved to be all too true.

What in fact seems to be the probable explanation for Saudi increases in production in late 1985 and early 1986 was a perceived change in the progress of the Iran-Iraq War. The Iraqi air offensive against Iranian oil targets seemed to be gaining in effectiveness, and at the same time pipelines were being completed that would take additional Iraqi oil through Saudi Arabia. Thus we see increases in Saudi and Iraqi production to make up for any losses caused by a dramatic drop in prices, while at the same time Iraqi attacks were at least keeping Iran from increasing its production.

This suggests that Saudi oil policy was intimately linked with the political environment, and balance of power, in the Gulf and in the Middle East, and was in this case being used as a political weapon against Iran. It appears that Saudi Arabian oil policy is driven by more than economic interest narrowly understood, but by a combination of Saudi economic and

---

3   Petroleum Intelligence Weekly, March 1, 1982.

Saudi Arabian Oil Policy and the Iran-Iraq War

political long-term goals, and the political climate within which such policy must operate. Because of Saudi weakness and lack of internal cohesion, Saudi Arabia has often Failed to pursue policies which it conceives of as in its long-term interests. often the Saudis are put into situations that pose overwhelming dangers as in 1979 and 1982, or as in August 1986, they place themselves into a role which they lack the strength to continue. Either way, this helps to explain Saudi behavior which many times may seem economically perverse and counter-productive.

Chapter 2: Oil Price Theory

Overview

The best method of analyzing the fundamental inconsistency of Saudi Arabian oil policy is to first discern what is the long-term economic policy that, theoretically, an economically rational Saudi Arabia would follow. Then one must review the actual history of Saudi Arabian oil policy to determine if it is in fact economically rational. If it proves to be other than economically rational as I propose, then one must try to develop a theory that better explains and reconciles the differences between Saudi Arabia's economic latitude and the political atmosphere which hinders this latitude. This chapter examines Saudi economic interests and how they have not been met by Saudi oil policy.

The Dominant Producer and Economic self-interest

Economic studies suggest that OPEC pricing structure and Saudi Arabian oil policy can be predicted using economic forecasting based on self-interest. The assumption is that Saudi Arabia and OPEC are economically rational, and act in the interest of setting a price that maximizes revenue. As dominant producer, Saudi Arabia is responsible for deciding what is the best course for OPEC policies to follow, and then enforcing this decision.

Saudi Arabian Oil Policy and the Iran-Iraq War

Maximizing revenue, in the case of a non-renewable resource, entails not just receiving the best price for one's product, but also insuring that one's assets are managed such that their appreciation potential is fully realized for future gains. In other words, if the producer believes that while considering the depreciation allowance for unrealized gains, the product will be worth more in the future, then production and sale of such product should be delayed, or, in the case of oil, kept in the ground. Also, it demands that the producer not charge a price so high as to attract competitors, or to drive consumers to replacement.

Arguments are made that just such economic self-interest insures that Saudi Arabia and OPEC will take no actions that will obviously harm the international economy on the grounds that future oil sales are based on the health of the industrial countries economies. Eliyahu Kanovsky claims that, "During the past 20 years, official declarations not withstanding, the Saudis have fairly consistently based their oil decisions primarily on what they have perceived to be their economic interest."[4] He claims that in the Fall of 1973, after the war, it was technical problems in the oil fields that caused the reduction in production and that production was back up to normal in the next quarter. He further observes that in 1974 with a depressed market, the Saudis kept production up, and in 1977, overproduced their ceiling. He also claims they kept production high, and prices low in 1979. The Saudis did this, according to Kanovsky, because they wanted to produce oil at moderate prices until they completed their modernization plans.[5]

---

4   Eliyahu Kanovsky, "On Saudi Oil Policy," <u>New York Times</u>, December 19, 1980, p. 35.
5   ibid.

Saudi Arabian Oil Policy and the Iran-Iraq War

Another line of thought suggests that the interdependence between Saudi Arabia and the financial institutions of the West preclude the Saudi's from taking actions that would damage Western economies since the Saudis have so much invested in the West that if the Western economies plummeted so too would their own investments.

These arguments, though logical and in many ways useful, have been proven on the whole to be incorrect by simple examination of Saudi actions, and those of OPEC in which the Saudis took part. This is due to the incorrect assumption that OPEC pricing is in large measure controlled by Saudi Arabia due to its overwhelming dominance in oil reserves and production capacity.

Saudi support of price increases has traditionally come when world economies were in deep recessions, and when demand was slack, thus defying the theory of economic self-interest and market strategy. Kanovsky pointed to the "technical difficulties" experienced by the Saudis, but as Quandt has observed:

> It seems implausible that the pattern of Saudi production between November 1973 and May 197 was primarily a function of technical problems. The source for this belief is an ARAMCO official testifying before a skeptical congressional committee... It must have been very convenient in such circumstances to have been able to argue that ARAMCO's hands were tied because of technical problems in the oil fields... there is little doubt that political considerations must be taken into account.[6]

---

6   William B. Quandt, Saudi Arabia's Oil Policy, (Washington, D.C.: The Brookings Institute, 1982), p. 1.

Kanovsky also stressed the Saudi's "high production, and low price" in 1979. In fact, in early 1979, at the height of the Iranian disruption:

> Saudi Arabia cut production from 10.to 8.0 mbd... by mid-February the <spot> price had jumped to over $31... Saudi Arabia 'led the regiment from behind,' keeping its own official price usually $2 or so below the price... of others.[7]

Such action does not reflect an economically moderate Saudi Arabia, but rather a country that is either duplicitously conspiring with its fellow producers, or forced into such action in an effort to appease radical political pressure.

OPEC Decision Making

Economically, OPEC decision making involves setting the price for a single grade of oil; light Arabian crude. The market then sets the price and quantity for the other grades. The initial price decision "is highly politicized and falls more appropriately into the political arena of legitimized action and issue priorities than in the economic realm of equilibrium theory."[8] Though Saudi Arabia, may seem economically much more flexible because of its limited need for revenue, it is actually very "vulnerable to cultural, ideological, and security pressures both inside and outside OPEC, (and thus) the government is by no means unilaterally able to set the world

---

7 Adelman in Dermot Gately, "A Ten-Year Retrospective: OPEC and the World Oil Market." Journal of Economic Literature, September 1984, p. 1103.
8 Charles f. Doran, "OPEC Structure and Cohesion: Exploring the Determinant of Cartel Policy." Journal of Politics, February 1980, p. 83.

price for petroleum in defiance of the preference of other members."[9]

Saudi Arabia is simply not strong enough, politically or militarily, to act as the dominant producer and enforce its own views of price moderation. Thus OPEC policy cannot be viewed as an extension of Saudi policy, and the vitally important political considerations of the area must be examined if one is to understand the true dynamics of OPEC pricing.

Economic Modeling

The modeling of OPEC behavior and thus Saudi Arabian behavior have in many instances been based solely on economic assumptions. These arguments explain that the 1973 oil price rise was entirely a function of economic rationality on the part of the producers. Thus future oil prices can be forecast by discovering the price that would best "maximize" the future revenue of the producers. Two arguments have been offered to explain how this worked: the first suggests that "OPEC effectively cartelized the world oil market, exploiting its power to raise prices above competitive levels by restricting production," and the second suggests "that OPEC was largely irrelevant," and that "the price increase merely reflected a shift in the underlying market conditions, in favor of OPEC, that had been occurring since the late 1960s."[10]

This analysis suggests that it was the economic interests involved in the decision that really counted. Whether OPEC acted out of the interest and intention of the oligopolist, or simply in reaction to market conditions that evidently took a

---
9   ibid., p. 83.
10 Gately, p. 1101.

swing in their favor, it is clear according to this argument that OPEC decision makers would be termed "economically rational." The actions of economically rational actors can be plotted mathematically using economic forecasts of the market. One only needs to accurately forecast future conditions.

Pindyck, in 1978, claimed that "OPEC's pricing behavior is surprisingly predictable, since the cartel is most likely to take only those actions that are in its best economic interest.... One must therefore put himself in OPEC's position and ask what is the best price to charge for oil."[11] That will more than likely be the price OPEC would charge.

The variables that one would use to come to the best price would be the maximizing of revenue, and maximizing of equity value of oil supplies. "Future revenues must be discounted to reflect income lost by not investing current revenue."[12] Thus, though the impact of positive price changes affects the development of alternate strategies to cope with increased oil prices very slowly, a rational OPEC would not radically increase prices in an effort to make a "quick killing." This is because the long run demand for OPEC oil would fall, and the future equity value of that oil would drop, along with OPEC revenue.

Another argument claims that OPEC may raise the price of oil on the grounds of conserving a valuable and non-renewable resource, but Pindyck maintains that, "overconservation is as bad as underconservation, since it simply reduces the net value of a resource to its owner. OPEC's problem is to exploit its resources in a way that balances revenue obtained from

---

11 Robert S. Pindyck, "OPEC's Threat to the West." Foreign Policy, Spring 1978b, p. 37.
12 ibid., p. 37.

current production with the discounted revenue that could be obtained from future production."[13]

Another aspect of OPEC behavior that must be balanced into the economic argument is the existence of a cartel rather than a monopoly that has a single depreciation rate. A cartel is made up of disparate economic interests that unite for the achievement of common goals. As it is defined in Griffin:

> The organizational architecture of a fully profit-maximizing cartel can be described as follows: the cartel will maximize profits by making each producer a member, and then allocating production among producers so that the marginal production costs are equalized among producers.[14]

The economic interests of one OPEC nation may differ from those of another on many important policy decisions. Yamani made this clear when he stated that because Algeria had limited natural reserves of oil, if he were the Algerians, he would:

> wish the price per barrel of oil to reach $100 this very day even at the risk of driving the world to an economic depression... And if by so doing I encourage and drive the world to invest in finding alternative sources of energy, such investments will not bear fruit in less than ten years, at which time the matter would be of no concern to me.[15]

---

13 ibid., pp. 38-39.
14 James M. Griffin, and David J. Teece, OPEC Behavior and World Oil Prices, (Boston: George Allen, & Unwin, 1982), p.25.
15 William B. Quandt, Saudi Arabia in the 1980s, (Washington, D.C.: The Brookings Institute, 1981), p. 168.

Saudi Arabian Oil Policy and the Iran-Iraq War

Cartel behavior entails neutralizing these tensions, and, universally within the cartel, adopting a common strategy and policy. Pindyck agrees that one of the problems for OPEC "is the fact that its membership is not homogeneous, but instead consists of countries that have somewhat different objectives and operate under different constraints."[16] He divides OPEC into two groups of countries: the "savers" and the "spenders". The "savers" are those countries characterized as having less immediate needs for cash, and tend to have large reserves of oil. Because of this, they value future oil revenue greatly. Pindyck includes Saudi Arabia, Kuwait, Libya, and U.A.E. in the "saver" class of OPEC members. The "spenders" are characterized as having greater immediate needs for revenue, and tend to have smaller reserves of oil. Thus, they prefer greater revenue now, when they have the oil, even if it means less demand later when their reserves may be virtually depleted.

The resolution of this internal conflict is what Pindyck sees as the central bargaining process inside OPEC. Between the two groups, Pindyck believes that "there is every reason to expect the interests of the saver countries to dominate, since they (and particularly Saudi Arabia) have the greatest production capacity and at the same time absorb most of the necessary production cutbacks."[17]

These arguments have, with time, proven to be false. OPEC, when looked upon as an oligopolistic institution set on maximizing long-term revenue, has proven to be irrational in that it raised prices and lowered its production beyond the point that the argument claims would be rational behavior. Indeed, as recent events have shown, OPEC did in fact price itself out of the market in exact opposition to the economic

---

16 Pindyck, p. 39.
17 ibid., p. 39.

argument. Indeed, by November of 1982, it was apparent that OPEC was losing its control of the market, with non-OPEC oil production outpacing OPEC by 20 mbd to OPEC's 18.2 mbd.[18]

Pindyck's argument that OPEC's cartel policy is also based on economic rationality has also proven to be false. Not only have the "saver" countries failed to dominate OPEC in such a role as he suggested, but they have often acted contrary to what the interests of a "saver" country implies. Libya, included as one of the "savers," has been a hard line price hawk, and Kuwait has often aligned itself with this block. Saudi Arabia, armed with its vast array of oil weapons to chastise and control its fellow members, has often declined to use these in favor of cooperating, albeit reluctantly, with the hawks within OPEC.

OPEC acts neither as an oligopoly out to maximize revenue, or as a cohesive economic cartel with the economically powerful members dominating the process of decision making. Instead, OPEC has often been driven by a political process that is often fundamentally economically irrational, and Saudi Arabia has gone along with it because they are politically unwilling or unable to control OPEC policy in the way that economic theories suggest they should.

The Political Model

According to Moran, Saudi Arabian oil policy is based on "an operational code of advancing Saudi political priorities while minimizing hostile external and internal pressures upon the Kingdom."[19] This suggests that instances where Saudi Arabia exercised price leadership were based on more than economic

---
18 Petroleum Intelligence Weekly, November 15, 1982.
19 Moran, p. 253.

calculations of market strength or the state of the World economy, but also on vital political concerns which price moderation served.

Such political factors that encourage moderate oil policy is the Saudi desire to limit the income of its more populace and militarily capable neighbors by keeping oil prices relatively low. This is because such countries as Iran and Iraq can more efficiently utilize their income to further develop their military, while Saudi Arabia, lacking most of the infrastructure, is at an extreme disadvantage on this level. A further political factor which promotes moderate oil prices is the Saudis desire to have close ties to the West. Price moderation is an economic boon to the West that encourages the West to reciprocate politically.

Price leadership in terms of of the political model is an economic tool that serves a political end. Its political definition is identical to that of the economic definition, in that it "refers to the explicit enunciation of future offering prices by the self-appointed 'leader' backed by a production policy that supports the announced offering prices, and accompanied by the maintenance of enough spare capacity to discipline cheaters or dissenters."[20] The actual exercise of this leadership is the central issue of Saudi Arabian oil policy.

The political model tries to deal with the fact that economic models fail to include the important variable of political reality. As Yamani pointed out, Algeria has different economic goals than Saudi Arabia, and for OPEC to succeed some compromise must be accomplished between the two. This is a decidedly political process. What must also be considered is that many of the OPEC countries that theoretically have similar economic interests similar to those

---

20 ibid., p. 254.

of Saudi Arabia, such as Libya, have markedly different political goals. The political model tells you when concern for economic factors is likely to be more important and when it will not. Thus, the political model encompasses the economic model, and shows that often economic consideration is pushed aside, within both OPEC and Saudi Arabia, and that conflicting political considerations of the dominant OPEC states are more often than not, the deciding factor for oil policy decisions.

The difficulty with the political model is that it lacks the crispness that is associated with economic models. Because it is often difficult, if not impossible, to quantify political security, and other political factors, the political model may seem to lack a predictive capacity. This may be true, but in reality no more so than the economic models. Though the political model may offer no concrete predictions on future oil policies of OPEC or Saudi Arabia, it does not make concrete economic forecasts that prove to be unpractical and untrue. Rather the political model tries to develop a true picture of the process of policy development. It accepts the economic realities of economic self-interests, but argues that often political considerations preclude a country or a body from following such a policy. In essence the political model strives for greater accuracy at the cost of precision, versus the economic model which is precise but inaccurate.

The very nature of such a political model creates an ambiguity that is inherent in the political system, but this is if anything a strong point. Understanding the true mechanisms of political decisions are valuable even if future forecast from such knowledge is ambiguous.

Saudi Arabian oil policy must be considered an economic/political tool that is in the hands of the Saudi government. This government is politically weak and vulnerable to its powerful neighbors. One can hardly expect that such an important issue as oil, can somehow remain aloof from the political turmoil that is part of the Middle East. Thus, to really understand the factors of oil policy decisions, one must understand the political atmosphere of the Middle East, one of the most contentious of all possible topics. The following chapters will strive to explain Saudi Arabian oil policy in the context of the Middle Eastern political atmosphere.

Chapter 3: The 1970s

Overview

Traditionally Saudi Arabia maintained that oil had no political purpose. Above all, it denied that the "oil weapon" could be used to achieve Arab political goals. Yet in 1973 the Saudis did just that: used the unusable oil weapon. This ambivalent view towards oil as a political tool reflected the belief held by the Saudis before then that a steep increase in the price of oil would result in an equally precipitous investment policy by the West to develop alternative sources of energy, and greater conservation measures that would in the long run eliminate, or lessen, OPEC and Saudi Arabia as the primary producers of oil in the world. It also reflected a political goal not to alienate the United States.

Twice in the 1970s, Saudi Arabia actions resulted in precipitous increases in the price of oil. First, in 1973 during the October War between Israel and the Arab states lead by Egypt, and secondly, in 1979 when the Iranian Revolution was then in full swing and Camp David had removed Egypt from the Arab political fold. In both these cases, one must say that Saudi actions could only be considered perverse when examined from the economic perspective. In the first instance, Saudi oil policy became a tool to further Saudi political interests, and in the second instance it was used to appease radical interests within OPEC.

Saudi Arabian Oil Policy and the Iran-Iraq War

The 1973 Oil Embargo and aftermath

In 1973, the Saudis had felt pressure to increase production because of increased world demand, and had consistently been encouraging ARAMCO to do so. The year before Saudi Arabia had increased production in response to the same pressure. At this time in early 1973, tension was also building between Israel and the surrounding Arab states. Warnings made by the Saudis that potential conflict in the area could result in a cut off of oil supplies were ignored by the State Department, which took them not as an authentic Saudi concern, but "as either empty rhetoric or unsophisticated attempts at blackmail."[21]

When the war broke out on October 6, 1973, the Saudis at first made no cuts in their production. They allowed ARAMCO to carry on production as if it was "business as usual." By October 13, the United States was beginning to airlift supplies to the Israelis, and still Saudi Arabia did nothing. On October 16, OPEC met in Kuwait to raise posted prices of OPEC oil, and Saudi Arabia went along. The next day a five percent decrease in production was added to the measure. Saudi Arabia, though agreeing to the reduction at the meeting, only reduced its production by two percent.[22] On October 19, President Nixon called for the Congress to give $2.2 billion in aid to Israel for arms and expenses. The same day, the Egyptian high command was shown Russian reconnaissance photographs indicating that Israeli armor had crossed the Suez canal in force, and was threatening to destroy Egypt's Third Army.[23] The next day Saudi Arabia,

---

21 Quandt, Saudi Arabia's Oil Policy, p. 10.
22 David B. Golub, When Oil and Politics Mix: Saudi Oil Policy. 1973-1985, (Cambridge, Massachusetts: Center for Middle Eastern Studies, Harvard University, 1985), p. 11.
23 ibid., p. 12.

along with the rest of OPEC, declared an embargo of oil shipments to the United States and the Netherlands.[24] It was not until Sadat seemed in serious danger of losing the war did the Saudis declare its acceptance of the Embargo.

More important than the actual embargo was the accompanying cut in production in October and early November which gave the action teeth. OPEC threatened that it would cut production below the September 1973 level steadily until Israel withdrew from occupied Arab territory. The plan was revised, but most Arab countries made coordinated production cuts, and a temporary shortage began to develop on the international oil market driving up the price of oil.

Negotiations began, and by May 1974, with the completion of the disengagement negotiations between Israel and Syria, the Embargo officially came to and end, and normal levels of production resumed.

In explaining Saudi actions during the oil embargo, the argument of economic interest does not stand up. The Saudis had previously seen their interests lying in keeping a moderate oil policy on the grounds of insuring a future market for their oil. Time has shown that the Saudi Arabian concern over increasing oil prices was well justified. Indeed, with the increase in oil prices in 1973 came a massive increase in Western efforts to gain energy independence through the development of alternate forms of energy and increasing conservation. These efforts have proven to be very successful, and have severely weakened OPEC influence.

If one considers only the economic side of the issue one may declare that Saudi Arabia's participation in the oil embargo

---

24 Quandt, Saudi Arabia's Oil Policy, p. 10.

was a mistake caused by a failure of the Saudis to fully calculate their self-interest. Though the decision may have been economically irrational, it was not poorly calculated. The Saudis thought long and hard on the matter, and tried in many ways to delay their participation in the embargo. Only until the Egyptian forces seemed in serious danger, did the Saudis actually institute serious cuts. Thus, although it was done with great reluctance, Saudi Arabia used its oil production as a political tool to support Sadat, and a political power structure in the Middle East which Saudi Arabia felt was important to its security. If the war had resulted in a defeat of Egyptian forces, Sadat would have fallen, and in his place may have arose a radical anti-Western leader which would have threatened the conservative Arab states in the same way as Nasser.

The argument that Saudi Arabian output was reduced due to technical problems, and that the embargo was simply staged to cover these difficulties up, as stated before, seem dubious at best. The fact that the embargo started when the Saudis realized that Israel had militarily turned the tide against Egypt, and then ended when hostilities were officially ended suggests that more than coincidental technical problems were involved in the cut-back of Saudi oil production.

Rather, Saudi Arabia chose to follow an economically irrational course of action in an effort to further what it perceived as its political interests. With Egypt on the verge of a military disaster, Saudi Arabia could hardly resist requests pressed by Sadat, a fellow moderate Arab leader, to impose an embargo in order to pressure the United States into a more pro-Egyptian stand. As Quandt suggests:

> It is hard to imagine that the Saudis could have remained totally indifferent to Arab opinion...

> According to non-Saudi observers in the kingdom at the time, the announcement of the embargo and the production cuts was greeted with overwhelming popular greeted.[25]

Not only were Saudi political interests served by the embargo, in that it seemingly forced the United States to restrain Israel, there were great external and internal political pressures on the Saudis to participate in the embargo. Failure to cooperate with their Arab neighbors could have resulted in internal disorder and potential sabotage of the Saudi oil fields.

Security interests seemed to suggest that Saudi Arabia could not afford to be passive. As it was, the Saudi decision to participate actively in the embargo "ensured King Faisal a place of unchallenged prominence as an

Arab and Saudi leader."[26] It also successfully supported Saudi goals of creating a more pro-Western alignment in the Middle East. Through the Damascus, Cairo, Riyadh bloc cemented by the war, and with the backing of the United States, Saudi Arabia hoped to bring long-term solutions to the problems in the Middle East.

The crisis of 1973 represents the first time that Saudi Arabia abandoned its economic interests in favor of using its oil resources in an effort to reduce political threats to the regime.

---

25 Quandt, Saudi Arabia's Oil Policy, p. 12.
26 ibid., p. 12.

Moderation between 1974 to 1979

In December 1973, a price high of $10 per barrel was set, effectively quadrupling prices within a one year period. By January 1974, Saudi Arabia's oil minister declared that Saudi Arabia "would move to reduce oil prices to ease adverse effects on the world economy."[27] For the Saudis, higher prices were politically injurious as well as economically. The Saudis did not want the Shah of Iran to become too powerful, and they further did not want to threaten their ties with the United States. The Saudi's planned to reduce oil prices by holding a large auction sale which would hopefully drive down the price of oil. Due to regional political pressure, the Saudis never actually held their oil auction, and instead allowed the price to stay at the price agreed upon in Tehran:

> The immediate reason For not pressing with the auction was the fear of antagonizing Iran, whose ruler had declared he would consider any action to bring down the price of oil as a hostile act. Another motive was to avoid provoking Iraq and other Arab producers, especially since an important Arab summit was scheduled to meet in Rabat in October 1974.[28]

Though the Saudis agreed to accept the higher prices resulting from the Embargo, despite their negative ramifications for Saudi Arabia, they fought against any further price hikes. Between the price hikes of 1973, and the incredible price explosion in 1979, the Saudis Followed a pattern of action more consistent with the economic self-interest model

---

[27] Nadav Safran, Saudi Arabia: The Ceaseless Quest for Security, (Cambridge, Massachusetts: The Belknap Press of Harvard University Press, 1985), p. 168.
[28] ibid., p. 170.

Saudi Arabian Oil Policy and the Iran-Iraq War

suggested for a country that is the largest producer in OPEC, with the largest known reserves in the world. Saudi Arabia kept production at levels supporting the OPEC price structure, but fought to keep prices stable and increases only marginal. In fact, due to inflation, the real price of oil in dollar terms was actually declining. At Doha in 1976, the Saudis and the U.A.E. broke with the rest of OPEC, agreeing to a price hike of only five percent compared to the ten percent desired by the rest of OPEC. Saudi production soared to a level of 9 mbd throughout 1977 in an effort to enforce moderation in price policy upon OPEC. By the middle of 1977, OPEC met and Saudi Arabia agreed to another five percent price increase to be followed by a price freeze by the other members. This accomplished, the price of Arabian light crude stayed at $12.70 per barrel for the next year and a half, and spot prices were virtually identical to OPEC contract prices suggesting an equilibrium of the market at this price.

The Saudis were able to succeed in their efforts to stabilize the market largely due to the political climate of stability. after the 1973 war, the Middle Eastern power structure was more favorable to Saudi Arabian political interests than at any time before. after the October War, Egypt moved closer to the West, and thus protected the Saudis on their western flank. Iran, though often a competitor for Persian Gulf hegemony, protected Saudi Arabia on its Eastern flank against Iraq. Furthermore, the Saudis succeeded during this period because they had the prestige associated with the 'victory' in 1973.

These efforts by Saudi Arabia to stabilize the market were not to be lasting. In 1978, the combined setbacks of the fall of the Shah of Iran, and the ostracism of Egypt due to Camp David, thrust the Middle East into turmoil, and severely reduced the abilities of Saudi Arabia to control OPEC. Saudi Arabia was left virtually politically alone.

1978 and the Price Increases of 1979

1978 was a time of great confusion for Saudi Arabia. During this period the Saudis had to deal with the Iranian revolution on the one hand, and the rise of a new and dangerous Ba'athist unity between Iraq and Syria on the other. To complicate matters the radicals in the Arab bloc, led by Iraq and Syria, were putting severe pressure on the Saudis to ostracize Egypt because of the Camp David agreement.

Though the Iran of the Shah had been a potentially ominous rival for Gulf hegemony, the Shah had also been a powerful check upon Iraqi ambitions in the Gulf. With the loss of the Shah, revolutionary Iran was now a danger that menaced the conservative governments of the Gulf, and destroyed the balance of power that had been represented by the triangle of Baghdad, Riyadh, and Tehran. Iraq was now free to vie for the hegemonic leadership of the Arab world without external restraint, and was the main instigator against Egypt and the Camp David accords.

Faced with a plethora of conflicting obligations and challenges, Saudi Arabia tried to deal with each issue in a piece-meal fashion that failed in the end to produce any real security. The Saudis tried to appease the new Islamic regime in Iran by stressing their shared devotion to Islamic principles, and by modifying Saudi policies, especially those concerning oil. They further aligned themselves with Iraq and Syria by adopting an anti-Camp David stance. The Saudis hoped that they could maintain their American support without losing their Arab block support, and also oppose any Iranian aggression or subversion without looking too pro-Western. Unable to decide where to turn, or who to turn to, Saudi policy lacked consistency throughout this period.

Saudi Arabian Oil Policy and the Iran-Iraq War

The Iranian revolution not only caused a total reversal of previous Saudi efforts to achieve a balance of power in the Gulf, it also struck a crippling blow to earlier Saudi efforts to stabilize the world oil market. In 1978, Iranian oil production began to fall with the disruption caused by the Iranian revolution. When the prices on the spot market jumped from $13 to $19 between October and November, Saudi Arabia began to raise its production to its maximum level of a little over 10 mbd in order to keep prices from going out of control. Saudi Arabia clearly saw its interests lying in a stabilized oil market.

By late 1978 and early 1979, this had all changed. At the OPEC meeting in Abu Dhabi in December 1978, OPEC decided to adopt a policy of making quarterly adjustments to OPEC prices in order to raise prices. This reflected the agenda of Baghdad I which set a more radical tone in both regional politics and in oil.

> With Iran as an uncertain source of regional support, the Saudis felt increasing pressure to seek better relations with Iraq, the Gulf's next most powerful actor... In effect, the Saudis accepted the price hike at Abu Dhabi for the same reasons that it accepted the unpublished sanctions at Baghdad I.[29]

Political considerations had Forced Saudi Arabia to abandon its support for Egypt, and also caused it to support OPEC radicals in their efforts to raise prices.

The policy shift of greatest importance was Saudi Arabia's decision to cut its production at two critical periods in 1979. In January 1979, Saudi Arabia initiated its first production cutback, setting a ceiling of 9.5 mbd for the first quarter. The

---
29 Golub, pp. 29-30.

Saudi Arabian Oil Policy and the Iran-Iraq War

resulting cancellation of contracts forced the spot market prices up from $16 per barrel to over $22. Then in April, when the spot market was beginning to soften somewhat, the Saudis declared further cutbacks from 9.5 mbd down to 8.5 mbd. Spot prices reached $29 per barrel in May, and $35 in June.[30]

Some suggest that what caused the price hikes of 1979 were actually uncertainties as to the new Iranian regime's plans for future production. This does not fully explain the dramatic increase in price that took place during this period. The uncertainty as to future levels of Iranian production suggests that:

> Some long-term price increase was thus inevitable. But the loss of perhaps 2 million to 3 million bpd of Iranian production cannot account by itself for the magnitude of the 1979-80 price hikes.[31]

What does account for this increase in price were the production policies of Saudi Arabia. After spending a number of years following the 1973 price hike fighting to keep oil price at moderate levels, the Saudis cut production during the most critical period of the Iranian oil production cut-off, causing massive jumps in the price of oil on the spot market. If they had chosen, the Saudis could have kept the price of oil at reasonable levels during this period by keeping their production up, and declaring the intention of expanding production further if necessary. Instead the Saudis chose to destroy all the effort of years of moderation in less than six months.

---

30 Quandt, Saudi Arabia's Oil Policy, p. 17.
31 ibid., p. 16.

Saudi Arabian Oil Policy and the Iran-Iraq War

Quandt gives many potential reasons for this odd behavior by the Saudis. One is that the Saudis sought price increases in an effort to correct cash flow problems encountered in 1977 and 1978. It seems unlikely that this is the reason, for with the price increases installed in December 1978 a modest surplus would have been acquired. There was no pressing financial need for the incredible increases that actually took place. "In addition," as Quandt points out, "if the Saudis simply wanted more income, the easiest way to have gotten it in 1979 would have been to raise prices in June to $24 per barrel, as the rest of OPEC did."[32]

The second explanation offered by Quandt is the possibility that technical problems caused the Saudi cuts in production. If this were the case the ceiling posted by Saudi Arabia would have been unnecessary. It was as much the declaration of the cutbacks as the cutbacks themselves that fueled the speculative price hike.

The third explanations suggests that "the Saudis simply made an error in view of their long-term interests."[33] When Iranian production came back onto the market, they incorrectly believed their cut backs would have little effect. By not properly calculating the effect of increased commercial stockpiling, the Saudis underestimated the potential short term demand for oil. Quandt says, "The Saudis may be excused for not fully understanding this pattern... Still, the Saudis could read the signs from the spot market... If they had been seriously determined to correct their misreading of the market, they had ample opportunity to do so in May and June 1979."[34]

---

32 ibid., pp. 17-18.
33 ibid,. p. 18.
34 ibid., pp. 18-19.

Saudi Arabian Oil Policy and the Iran-Iraq War

What seems to be the more likely explanation for the Saudi production cuts is that the political situation did not allow it to follow a more moderate and desirable policy. In December 1976, Saudi Arabia was able to successfully challenge OPEC at Doha, and thus kept real oil prices relatively low, but in 1978 and 1979, Saudi Arabia was simply unwilling to stand up to a virtually united OPEC to ensure a more moderate oil policy:

> In December 1976 the regime was confident that its good relations with Cairo, Damascus, and Washington provided it with ample protection against then-present external threats. By December 1978, however, the threats had multiplied and the security configuration had all but collapsed. The regime's actions were, in this sense, a response to changes in the regional balance of power – changes set in motion by three roughly concurrent events: Sadat's signing of the Camp David accords on September 17, 1978; the incipient political crisis in Iran; and the announcement of Syrian-Iraqi unity plans on October 26.[35]

In this environment, it is understandable that Saudi Arabia cut its production on January 20, 1979, when only four days earlier the Shah had been forced to leave Iran. The Shah's exile ended any possibility of a more pro-Western regime coming into Iran, and forced Saudi Arabia to take a more conciliatory position toward regional radicals on a number of issues, including oil.

The Saudi actions of early 1979 are direct examples of Saudi Arabia abandoning its economic and political long-term interests in response to what it perceived as short-term

---
35 Golub, p. 29.

dangers. In this case it was a combination of the challenge that the new Islamic regime in Iran posed for Saudi Arabia and the other conservative Gulf states, and the pressure applied by the hard-line Iraqi-Syrian alliance. If they had chosen to do so, the Saudis could have kept the price of oil at reasonable levels during this period by keeping their production up, and declaring the intention of expanding production further if necessary, (in fact Saudi Arabia secretly increased its productive capacity anyway, but did not publicize this until April, 1980)[36] but this would have required a head on collision with the radicals in OPEC and in the Middle East. Instead the Saudis chose to abandon their previous oil policy positions and support the hard-line stance of the radical block.

Summer 1979 to the Iran-Iraq War

One can say that in 1979, Saudi Arabia was more or less forced to subsume its economic interests in the face of political exigencies. Its fear of Iran and its fear of Arab radicals forced the Saudis to abandon economic rationality and their long-term political planning, but by late 1979 and early 1980, another change occurred in Saudi policy. With the breakup of the Iraqi-Syrian alliance by the end of the summer of 1979, the growing tension between Iran and Iraq, and the December 1979 Soviet invasion of Afghanistan, which gave Saudi Arabia leverage in isolating the Russian supported and Syrian led radical element, Saudi Arabia was able to return to a more moderate course of action in regards to oil policy, and in its general political policy as well.

In July 1979, Saudi Arabia raised its production to 9.8 mbd and kept it at this rate for more than a year. They did this in

---
36 ibid., p. 29.

the face of a fading demand for OPEC oil, and dropping spot prices.[37] This Saudi action can be seen as an effort to repair the damage they had done earlier in the year. It was certainly in the Saudis interest to reverse the trends that were started by their previous cuts in production. What is truly significant is that the Saudis were able to succeed, whereas only months before they chose to capitulate to radical demands.

Part of what gave the Saudis their leeway was a series of short-term reverses experienced by the radicals in the Arab world, and Iraq's increasing preoccupation with Iran. This contributed to the somewhat successful Saudi efforts to isolate Syria and neutralizing Iran. Though Iraq did not provide the same conservative protection as the Shah due to the Shah's American support, Iraq did provide a limited check against Syrian and Iranian pressure.

The disintegration of the Baghdad-Damascus axis, which occurred in the summer of 1979, allowed Saudi Arabia to successfully follow a more moderate oil policy. The Syrians, pressing for more radical and stringent measures against the United States as well as Egypt, in November 1979 revived the "Steadfastness Front" which was composed of Syria, Libya, Algeria,

PDRY, and the PLO. This represented "an advanced degree of deterioration in Iraqi-Syrian relations in the consensus politics of the Baghdad conferences."[38] It also gave the Saudis an opportunity to play the Syrians and the Iraqis off against each other to buy themselves time. Iraqi-Iranian tensions were also rising, thus increasingly tying Iraq up with Iran, and leaving Saudi Arabia relatively unhindered.

---

37 Quandt, Saudi Arabia's Oil Policy, p. 14.
38 Safran, p. 316.

Saudi Arabian Oil Policy and the Iran-Iraq War

Another opportunity which Saudi Arabia took advantage of was the Soviet invasion of Afghanistan in December of 1979. Though this represented a grave threat to what the Saudis felt to be part of their security interests in the area, namely to keep Soviet influence at a minimum, it also represented an opportunity to further isolate pro-Soviet Syria and the Steadfastness Front by down-grading the Soviets in the eyes of Muslims in general, and Arabs in particular.

In January of 1980, Saudi Arabia called a meeting of the Islamic Conference to deal with the problem of Afghanistan. after making certain concessions to the radicals, the Islamic Conference met and discussed Afghanistan as the central issue. The Saudis hoped to be able to weaken the Soviet Union and its client states by discrediting the image of the Soviet Union as:

> the selfless friend of Arab and Muslim peoples and at least put those who would cooperate with it (the Soviet Union) in no better position than those who cooperated with the United States.[39]

Saudi oil policy in late 1979 and early 1980 reflected this general improvement in the political environment in favor of the Saudis. Saudi Arabia was able to press for greater moderation in oil policy, and kept its production up in virtual defiance of the radical element within OPEC. As the demand for oil was falling throughout 1980, Saudi production held at a high of 9.8 mbd. Also, the Saudis were able to dramatically increase their share of the market from 32 percent in late 1979 to 44 percent in October 1980.[40]

---

39 ibid., p. 320.
40 Quandt, Saudi Arabia's Oil Policy, p. 21.

Saudi Arabian Oil Policy and the Iran-Iraq War

Although OPEC contract prices rose from $2r at the start of 1980 to $26, then $28, and then $30 by August and September, spot prices had fallen from $38 in the beginning of 1980 to close to $32 in August and September.[41] This was the first time in two years that the spot prices and the contract prices were virtually equal, and reflected growing Saudi influence in oil policy. If the Iran-Iraq War had not broken out, disrupting large quantities of oil exports from both

Iran and Iraq, oil prices may very well have fallen yet further.

Though the Saudis were still forced to use Egypt as a rhetorical foil against the Syrians, distancing themselves from the Egyptians in an effort to prove to the Syrians and the rest of the Arab world that they were not "lackeys" to American "imperialism," the situation during this period changed slightly in favor of the Saudis. Indeed, as early as the latter part of 1979, Iraq was beginning to be more disposed to moderation on many grounds and was taking on the role of a virtual shield against Iran, and a check against Syria. In the area of oil, the Saudis were successful in their efforts to create a glut that forced fellow OPEC members to lower prices, and contributed to more stability in the world oil market.

By September 1980, the high levels of Saudi production that had been sustained throughout the year seemed to have paid off for them in OPEC politics. At the Vienna OPEC meeting in September, on the eve of the Iran-Iraq War, OPEC agreed to important concessions to Saudi Arabia. Saudi Arabia would raise the price of its marker crude to $30 on the condition that others effect price cuts from $32 per barrel to $30. This was at a time when spot prices were at around thirty-two dollars a barrel.[42]

---

41 ibid., p. 14.
42 ibid., p. 21.

Saudi Arabian Oil Policy and the Iran-Iraq War

The outbreak of the Iran-Iraq War negated this agreement, because the war had the effect of cutting off Iranian and Iraqi production. Spot prices shot up to over $40 per barrel, and Saudi Arabian oil production again increased to a maximum level of 10.3 mbd in order to make up for the loss of Iranian and Iraqi production.

Saudi Arabian Oil Policy and the Iran-Iraq War

Chapter 4: The Iran-Iraq War – September 1980 to March 1982

Overview

The period from the summer of 1979 through to the summer of 1982, represents a distinct period in Saudi Arabian oil policy. During this period Saudi Arabia acted as the main proponent of price moderation within OPEC. This followed a short but critical period in which Saudi Arabia had pursued a policy of limiting production, and supporting an OPEC push for higher prices. In an effort to force the rest of OPEC to hold to a more moderate pricing system, Saudi Arabia began a policy of over-producing that at one point took it to its maximum level of over 10 mbd. They were able to do this for two important factors associated with the Iran-Iraq War: 1. the quick development of the war into a stalemate, and 2. the protection offered by the United States in the form of fully manned AWACs. Then, in the summer of 1982, Saudi Arabia drastically reversed itself, and began again supporting OPEC pricing policy by adopting the onerous role of the "swing producer."

Their are two basic arguments to explain why Saudi Arabia changed its policy of confrontation with the OPEC radicals, and reverted back to a policy of conciliation. Some would suggest that it was because Saudi Arabia had achieved most of its goals and was looking to consolidate its victory by taking on the "leadership" role of "swing-producer." The most notable among these is William Quandt. The other argument suggests that Saudi Arabia abandoned its policy of moderate oil prices in the face Iranian pressure. The latter will be the argument put forward in this chapter.

The Swing Producer as OPEC Leader

In defending his argument, Quandt notes that Saudi Arabia began lowering its production in late 1981 after OPEC had agreed to Saudi demands for price unification, and by March 1982, seemed to be working to defend the $34 a barrel OPEC price that it had previously been attacking.

At this time, there was an oil glut that made the actual spot prices of oil much lower; an oil glut that Saudi Arabia had helped to engineer. Quandt suggests that attaining OPEC price unity, more than moderate OPEC pricing, was Saudi Arabia's basic goal. According to this argument, by 1982, the other OPEC members were willing to lower their prices to meet the Saudis', and a compromise was adopted by all.

This argument is open to question. Why would Saudi Arabia be so concerned about having the OPEC price unified, if it was at a price that they had previously considered damaging to their long-term interests? The general consensus on Saudi Arabian economic self-interest is that they want a price that will give them all the short-term revenue they need without driving consumers to radical conservation or alternative sources of fuel.[43]

At $34 a barrel, this was not the case. The Saudis felt, along with many economists, that such a price was too high for Saudi long term interests. This is shown in the fact that the Saudis for two years increased their production so as to

---

43 An excellent economic explanation of this, though a flawed total analysis, can be found in <u>Foreign Policy</u>, Spring of 1978b, by Robert Pindyck.

Saudi Arabian Oil Policy and the Iran-Iraq War

impose a glut on the market and force the radicals within OPEC to back down on their demands for higher prices. It is therefore odd that after almost two years of following a path of over-producing far above normal production levels in an effort to create just such a glut of oil, the Saudis reversed themselves just when this policy seemed to be successful, and gave in to radical demands for Saudi cuts in production.

In order to explain this contradiction, one must view Saudi Arabian oil policy as an integral part of Saudi Arabian political policy. In 1981 and 1982, the most important issue for the Saudis was the threat posed by Iran. It was an issue that put a tremendous amount of pressure on a relatively weak Saudi Arabia.

If one examines closely the situation preceding the Iran-Iraq war and the war itself, and then follows Saudi Arabian oil policy through this same period, one finds a direct correlation between the political environment in which the Saudis operated and the oil policy they followed.

When pressed by forces they could not counteract, they took a more conciliatory stance in an effort to neutralize the radical threat by cutting their oil production and supporting OPEC radicals. The fact that the other OPEC members lowered their prices at a united $34 price level in the summer of 1981 reflects a weak market more than moderation within OPEC. That the Saudis' behavior follows this pattern in more than just oil policy is a strong indicator that politics and economics are inseparably combined in Gulf politics, and that Saudi Arabian oil policy cannot be explained by economics alone.The Iran-Iraq War

By September 1980, Saudi Arabian oil policy seemed to have been a complete success. Saudi Arabia's high production at

Saudi Arabian Oil Policy and the Iran-Iraq War

9.8 mbd was putting tremendous downward pressure on the oil market, and was making it very difficult for some of the more hawkish OPEC members even to sell their oil. At the September 1980 OPEC meeting in Vienna, it seemed as though Saudi Arabia had finally won in its battle for lower prices and a more stable market. On the spot market, Saudi high production had driven prices down from an all time high of $41.00 a barrel in November and December of 1979 to a more reasonable $32 a barrel in August of 1980,[44] and in Vienna, Saudi Arabia had convinced OPEC to lower its contract price per barrel for its marker crude from $32 to $30, thus unifying OPEC pricing at Saudi levels. In order to do this, Saudi Arabia held out to its fellow OPEC members the threat of continued high levels of Saudi Arabian oil production, and the enticement of lower Saudi production if OPEC agreed to cooperate with Saudi goals:

> The agreement on a unified price was set by Saudi Arabia as a precondition to cutting back its enormous output in response to pleas from other producers, particularly Iran, which is having difficulty selling its more expensive oil because of glut in the market that has developed in the last few months.[45]

In order to insure that the Vienna agreement was not broken, Saudi Arabia was not going to actually cut its production until the end of year in order to discourage cheating.

This all proved meaningless due to the September invasion of Iran by Iraq. The Iraqi war plans envisioned a short, sharp campaign against a demoralized and depleted Iranian army that would result in the fall of the Islamic Revolutionaries

---

44 Quandt, Saudi Arabia's Oil Policy, p. 14.
45 New York Times, September 18, 1980.

from power in Tehran, the ascension of Iraq as the hegemonic leader of the Persian Gulf, and possibly the Middle East. The Iraqi plans called for an initially devastating air attack against the Iranian air force while it was still on the ground. Simultaneously, armored columns were to roll up the east side of the disputed Shatt al'Arab waterway and capture key ports and towns in the Khuzistan area.

This offensive was designed to defeat once and for all the Iranian army, hopefully trigger secessions of outlying provinces, and put such pressure on Iran as to cause "a break down of will at the center"[46] before the far superior Iranian navy would have the opportunity to strike back at Iraq.

Iraq was unable to deliver the crushing blow, and instead got bogged down in a war of attrition against a larger and more populous foe that was determined to withstand its attack. The war removed dramatic amounts of both Iraqi and Iranian oil from the market due to war damage, and caused a surge in spot market prices up to $40 a barrel by November 1980.[47] The hard won Saudi successes at Vienna were now negated due to the growing strength in the spot market, and thus Saudi efforts were temporarily frustrated.

After a month of heavy fighting, it became obvious that the war had degenerated into a war of attrition, which stood in marked contrast to the rapid blitzkrieg envisioned by the Iraqi planners.

For the Saudis, this offered even more latitude in pursuing their policies, especially in regards to oil, but also caused a serious short-term dilemma. The disruption of Iranian and Iraqi oil supplies due to the war, and the accompanying spot

---

46 Safran, p. 365.
47 Quandt, Saudi Arabia's Oil Policy, p. 21.

price increases from around $32 a barrel in August and September of 1980, to around $40 a barrel in October, November, December, and January of 1981, caused a major reversal in previous Saudi success.[48] In response to this Saudi Arabia raised production from 9.8 mbd to its maximum capacity of 10.3 mbd. With both Iran and Iraq neutralized due to the stalemate, Saudi Arabia was able to continue with its policy of keeping production high in an effort to force price moderation throughout 1981.

This seemed to be working until the Iranian victories a year later changed the balance of power in the Gulf, in the Middle East, and in OPEC, and forced Saudi Arabia to reconsider its priorities.

Threats and Opportunities for Saudi Arabia

For Saudi Arabia, Iraq's failure to quickly and decisively defeat Iran spawned fears that the situation might lead to an escalation of the war that would entangle the entire Gulf. Specifically, Saudi Arabia feared reprisals from Iran for Saudi support of Iraq. Saudi oil facilities and exports were easy targets for Iran, if Iran so chose to attack them. With its offshore facilities defenseless, and the vulnerable Strait of Hormuz within virtual control of Iran, Saudi Arabia felt vulnerable against the unpredictable Iranian regime.

In response to these dangers, Saudi Arabia turned to the United States for support. From September 30 on, U.S. AWACs flew air patrol deterring any attacks upon Saudi Arabia. Two U.S. carrier task forces cruised the Arabian Sea as further deterrence upon Iran not to close the Straits or attack the Arab states of the Persian Gulf.[49] With the decisive

---
48 ibid., p. 14.
49 Laurie Ann Mylroie, <u>Regional Security After Empire: Saudi Arabia and the</u>

Saudi Arabian Oil Policy and the Iran-Iraq War

show of United States support, the Saudis were able to take advantage of the resulting stalemate between Iran and Iraq. The war:

> Facilitated Saudi action... once it appeared that the most serious of the war's potential dangers would not be realized – the conflict would not spread to the other Gulf states; Iraq would not win a quick victory; and Iran would not block navigation in the Gulf.[50]

The fact that two of Saudi Arabia's most dangerous and powerful neighbors were both neutralized by the other, left Saudi Arabia relatively free to pursue its goals on many fronts. As Safran notes:

> Once the urgent and critical threats raised by the failure of Iraq's war plans were met, the ensuing stalemate was potentially much more advantageous to the Saudis than an Iraqi victory would have been.[51]

Though the outbreak of the war disrupted the international spot market for oil and temporarily reversed Saudi efforts, it did not disrupt Saudi Arabia's long-term efforts at controlling OPEC.

Gulf, unpublished doctoral dissertation, Harvard University, 1985, p. 307.
50 ibid., p. 305.
51 Safran, pp. 367-368.

The Stalemate and Saudi Arabian Oil Policy through 1981

Facing a prolonged confrontation with Iran, Iraq had to deal with many problems. With the effective military blockade of the Shatt al'Arab waterway by Iran, Iraq faced serious difficulties in getting military and civilian supplies to its hinterland and battle front, and faced an even more serious problem in financing these purchases from its now greatly reduced revenue from oil exports. Down to below one million barrels a day from a previous high of three and a half million, Iraq had little money to pay for the costly war with Iran outside of its reserves which could not be expected to last long.

The Iraqis now found themselves dependent on their neighboring Arab states for aid. Iraq needed further access from Jordan to the already heavily taxed port of Aqaba in order to make up for the loss of its Gulf port of Fao, and the use of Saudi ports on the Red Sea as well.

Of even greater importance was the financial aid that Iraq began receiving from the oil producing Gulf states, especially Saudi Arabia and Kuwait. With the serious reduction in Iraqi production, Saudi Arabia began increasing oil production in an effort to make up for the loss of Iraqi and Iranian supplies to the market, and to further support Iraq. Under a production credit scheme, Saudi Arabia and Kuwait produced oil for Iraq from the Neutral Zone between Saudi Arabia and Kuwait.[52]

In the December OPEC 1980 meeting in Bali, Saudi Arabia went along with an increase in OPEC contract price from $30 to $32. This was in response to the unprecedented rise in the

---

52 ibid., p. 371.

spot market to $40 a barrel.⁵³ Though it was impossible for Saudi Arabia to keep the OPEC contract price from going to $32 a barrel, it did keep its production at around 10.5 mbd for an unprecedented period of time. Previously, Saudi Arabia had produced at such levels for only short periods of less than a few months, but after the outbreak of the Iran-Iraq War, Saudi Arabia kept its production at its maximum levels for almost an entire year.

Within a short time these high levels of production began to deflate the prices on the spot market. By February and March of 1981, daily spot prices averaged around $37.00 a barrel, and by June the spot market had fallen back to the $32 a barrel price it been hovering at before the start of the war.⁵⁴ It looked as if Saudi Arabia was again in a position to impose a more moderate oil policy upon OPEC.

The Islamic Conference and Iranian Resistance

As Iraq tried to prepare itself for a stalemated war, Iran turned to the offensive. The first of these offensives began in January 1981, and none of them were particularly effective in dislodging the Iraqis from their positions on Iranian soil. Iraqi offensives proved equally ineffective in pushing the Iranians out of strategic locations. As summer approached its end, it seemed that there was a "'balance of weakness': Iraq had failed to win Iranian acquiescence to a new territorial compromise while Iran's attempts to push the invader back had proved futile."⁵⁵

---

53 New York Times, December 16, 1980.
54 Quandt, Saudi Arabia's Oil Policy, p. 15.
55 Legum, Sheked, and Dishon, ed., The Middle East Contemporary Survey, 1980-81, p. 25.

Saudi Arabian Oil Policy and the Iran-Iraq War

In March, 1981, an Islamic Conference commission composed of the leaders of Bangladesh, Pakistan, Guinea, and the PLO presented both the Iranians and the Iraqis with a two part plan to end hostilities between the two Islamic countries.

Though the plan was greeted with a certain amount of support by the Iranian government led by the secular figure, the French trained economist, Abdul Hassan Bani Sadr, the Iranian Supreme Defense Council, made up mostly of Islamic revolutionaries, rejected the proposal and offered three preconditions that must be met for there to be peace:

1. The Algiers Agreement of 1975 must stand as the only valid authority to the Shatt al'Arab question,

2. The regime of Saddam Hussein must be punished for their aggression, and

3. Their must be an immediate unconditional withdrawal of Iraqi troops from Iran.[56]

These were conditions that were clearly unacceptable to the government of Iraq.

In late March, another proposal was made by the peace Commission, and this time Bani Sadr accepted it. Again, due to the hardliners within the Iran, the proposal was rejected, and the final condition was set "that Saddam Hussein must resign or be deposed as part of any settlement."[57]

This was significant because it marked a greater confidence on the part of Iran that it could successfully continue the war. Within the next few months, Bani Sadr was dismissed and impeached, and the radical Islamic hardliners were brought to

---
56 ibid., p. 355.
57 Safran, p. 372.

Saudi Arabian Oil Policy and the Iran-Iraq War

power. This ended any hope of having the stalemate peacefully resolved.

The new president, Raja'i, while addressing a visiting Non-aligned delegation mediating between Iran and Iraq, presented Iran's now united stance:

> [You] have not been very useful in clarifying the stance of the aggressor and the situation of the nation against which that aggression has taken place ... Allow me to reiterate with some pride what I said in the initial meetings: we shall decide the fate of the war on the battle field... As we value your lives and time, we regard these comings and goings as fruitless.[58]

The stalemate, compounded by Iranian intransigence, left the Saudis in an excellent position to follow its desired oil policy. For Saudi Arabia, the continuation of the war was in their best interests. Iraq at this time was so heavily dependent on Saudi Arabian financial aid that it had virtually no say in pricing policy. Also, due to its virtual lack of production, Iraq no longer had any real motivation to press for higher prices against Saudi wishes, especially since it was receiving aid from Saudi Arabia. Iran, though resistant, was also very weak and had little real influence over issues in the Middle East, or OPEC.

This situation allowed the Saudis to continue to flood the market with oil in its continued effort to bring down prices, and stabilize the market. In fact by August 1981, Saudi share of OPEC production was at fifty percent, up twenty percent over a one year period.[59] Though Iraq was not winning, the

---

58 MECS, 1980-81, p. 355.
59 Quandt, Saudi Arabia's Oil Policy, p. 14.

fact that Iran was pinned down gave Saudi Arabia and the other Gulf conservatives a great amount of leverage in OPEC. At the August OPEC meeting in Geneva, Sheik Zaki Yamani declared that Saudi Arabia would maintain the $32 per barrel price through 1984, and that there could possibly be other cuts within OPEC.[60]

Within a month, conditions on the battle field were to reverse this situation. In September Saudi Arabia in turn reversed itself and cut its production, and in October, Saudi Arabia went along with an increase in

OPEC prices. Though it is possible that the September reduction in Saudi crude production may have been linked to an OPEC compromise in August, the Saudis' acquiescence in October implies a reversal of Saudi policy, and a definite reconsideration of the issues by Saudi Arabia.

The Iranian Offensives of 1981-1982

In September the 'balance of weakness' was threatened by a series of four consecutive Iranian offensives, and a general reverse in the course of the war took place. At first the offensives were written off as unimportant, but soon the character of the war began to take the shape of Iranian initiatives followed by unsuccessful Iraqi efforts to absorb and react to these attacks. The Iranian successes led to a dramatic shift in the balance of power in favor of Iran.

For Saudi Arabia, this presented a whole new set of security concerns. Previously, Saudi Arabia had depended on Iraq to neutralize Iran, Israel to deter Syria, and the United States to provide a general regional backing for Saudi interests. Of these strategic blocks by far the most important was the first,

---
60 New York Times, August 22, 1981.

for without Iraq to hold back Iran Saudi Arabia would have been virtually helpless. The Iranian offensives threatened to totally overrun Iraq, and thus deprive Saudi Arabia of its only real defense against Iranian radicalism.

By March 1982, Saudi Arabian policy rested on trying to keep Iran from launching what it feared would be a crushing final offensive against Iraq. All of Saudi Arabia's political and economic tools and assets were brought to bear to try to persuade and deter just such an Iranian attack. Saudi Arabian oil policy thus became hostage once again to Saudi efforts to neutralize a regional threat through appeasement.

The first Iranian offensive occurred on September 27, 1981, when the Iranians cleared the Abadan-Ahwaz road and the Abadan-Bander-e-Mashur road, lifting the year long siege of embattled Abadan. This one-day attack was conspicuous for its surprise and the use of massive amounts of concentrated artillery by the Iranians. After lifting the Iraqi siege of Abadan, the Iranian offensive then proceeded to force the Iraqis from their bridgehead across the Karun River, from which the Iraqis had been able to put pressure on the Abadan area.

Though at first the success of the Iranian offensive was written off as strategically unimportant by the different regimes in the area, it was an augury of events yet to come and gave the Iranians important strategic positions on the Shatt al'Arab. The Iraqis derided the Iranian victories as "imaginary" and explained their "transfer" across the Karun River as only "temporary" so that the Iraqis could better take the initiative.[61] This Iraqi initiative never showed itself except possibly in sporadic air attacks in which Iraq's air force was by this time superior.

---
61 MECS, 1981-82 p. 311.

Saudi Arabian Oil Policy and the Iran-Iraq War

At the same time, the third Saudi engineered oil glut was finally taking shape and it became obvious that either Saudi Arabia was going to have to cut production, or the rest of OPEC was going to have to agree with Saudi Arabia and cut their prices. Prices in the spot market had fallen from their high of $41.25 per barrel in November 1980, to a more reasonable $32.00 per barrel in August 1981. Instead of a general reduction in prices by OPEC, in September Saudi Arabia under OPEC criticism, particularly from Iran, reduced its production down to 9.2 mbd, a cut of more than a million barrels per day.

In late October, an emergency meeting of OPEC ministers was held in Geneva, in which OPEC prices were unified at an increased price of $34 per barrel, and Saudi Arabia agreed to make further cuts of more than 500,000 barrels per day, down to 9.7 mbd, in order to support these higher prices.[62] It is at this point that Quandt suggests that Saudi Arabia, succeeding in its efforts toward price unification, agrees to take the "leadership" position within OPEC. In reality Saudi Arabia had come incredibly close to achieving its goals only to then abandon them in the face of political adversity. Saudi Arabia allowed Iran to assume the dominant position within OPEC. Though the Iranian victories at this point were not overwhelming, they were serious enough to force Saudi Arabia to back down somewhat, and reconsider its high production policy.

The second Iranian offensive came on November 29, 1981, in the northern sector of the southern front. Launched from its base in Susangerd, the Iranian offensive moved toward the Iraqi base of Bostan, driving a wedge between the two Iraqi sectors, one to the northwest facing Dezful, and the other to

---

62 New York Times, October 30 & 31, 1981.

Saudi Arabian Oil Policy and the Iran-Iraq War

the south, based in Khorramshahr. In this offensive the Iranians first began to utilize the practice of human wave attacks, in which massive columns of poorly equipped Revolutionary Guards would storm the Iraqi front lines seeking martyrdom in the service of their country and their religion. These attacks were devastatingly effective, and made inroads into the Iraqi lines that allowed regular Iranian military units to advance "employing more conventional methods."[63]

The Saudis, now beginning to truly worry about the path of the war, chose to make further production cuts in November down to 8.6 mbd. With worries over the war prominent, and reduced Saudi output, spot prices began to inch back up to the $34 per barrel level. As the months passed Saudi production continued to fall in anticipation of another massive Iranian offensive in the Spring, but also due to OPEC pressure to support a lagging spot market. At $34 a barrel demand was sliding fast. Rather than offering discounts, which many other OPEC members were doing, Saudi Arabia resigned itself to lower levels of production in an effort to appease the now menacing Iran.

On December 13, 1981, Bahrain announced it had uncovered a major Iranian-instigated plot to topple the government of Bahrain. This was only one week after Iran's successful Bostan offensive and

> demonstrated to the Saudis the intent of Iran's ruling Islamic revolutionaries to go beyond the war of words and to export their revolution by instigating terrorism and subversion.[64]

---

63 MECS, 1981-82, p. 311.
64 Safran, p. 379.

Saudi Arabian Oil Policy and the Iran-Iraq War

It showed very clearly to Saudi Arabia the threat that Iran posed.

By March 1982, Saudi production reached a four year low of 7.1 mbd. On March 19, 1982, at the OPEC meeting in Vienna, amidst a falling oil market, Saudi Arabia officially lowered its production ceiling down to 7.5 mbd for March, and 7.0 mbd for April with a Saudi guarantee of lowering production further if that proved necessary to maintain the stated OPEC price.

It is at this point that Saudi Arabian oil policy became subservient to OPEC demands. Saudi Arabia made an about-face, and vowed to support a price that only months before it had attacked as short-sighted. "Thirty-four dollars is the marker crude price decided by OPEC," said Saudi Arabian oil minister Yamani, "If it is necessary to impose the lowest ceiling of the seven million barrels we will do that."[65] It is during this meeting that Saudi Arabia began to perform the role of "swing producer" propping up a price structure that it considered too high by cutting into its own oil production, though it was actually a year later when Saudi Arabia formally adopted the title.

The next Iranian offensive occurred on March 22, 1982. Greater in scale than the previous offensives, Operation Fath ("Conquest" or "Triumph") was a pincer movement based from the central front against the Iraqi 4th Army Corps along the Karkheh River line. This offensive "in three successive efforts – on 22, 24, 27

March... crippled three of the enemy divisions and cleared the Iraqi-occupied part of Khuzistan west and north of the

---

65 New York Times, March 21, 1982.

Karkheh, right up to the frontier."⁶⁶ The Iraqis at this point were saved from a total rout by the general exhaustion of the Iranian forces.

The fourth Iranian offensive began a month later on April 30, 1982, with another pincer attack, this time moving southward from Susangerd and south-west from the Ahwaz sector along the Ahwaz-Khorramshahr highway. This offensive was aimed at staking the pot city of Khorramshahr which had been held by the Iraqis since the beginning of the war, which the Iranians had renamed, Khuninshahr, or City of Blood.⁶⁷

After initial success in crossing the Karun River and capturing many Iraqi prisoners, the Iranians began meeting fierce resistance. Continuing with the attack, Iranian forces pressed forward and captured many important Iraqi military posts, including the junction of the Ahwaz-Khorramshahr road and the Basra road. Taking the secondary road towards Basra, the Iranian forces reached the frontier, and dug in North of Khorramshahr.

In the second phase of the offensive, on May 21, 1982, Iranian forces began to move against Iraqi held Khorramshahr. Within two days, they had broken through the Iraqi defense of minefields and trenches. The next day, the twenty-fourth day of the offensive, Iranian forces recaptured the city. Iraqi forces attempted to evacuate, but with heavy casualties. In the fight for Khorramshahr, "according to Iranian reports, 30,000 Iraqis were captured in a battle that essentially terminated the Iraqi invasion of Iran."⁶⁸ The loss of Khorramshahr stood as the worst Iraqi defeat up to that time, and provided the low water mark for Iraqi fortunes.

---

66 MECS, 1981-82, p. 311.
67 Ibid., p. 311.
68 Safran, p. 383.

This series of Iranian offensives, which began as an "insignificant" Iranian victory at Abadan resulted in a general expulsion of the Iraqi presence from Iran.

The Iraqi Withdrawal

By this point the erosion Saudi Arabia's commitment to price moderation totally ended. The Saudis were feeling very pressed, and were looking in all directions for any means to save the situation from total ruin.

With the stunning defeat of Iraq, worries began to surface about whether Saddam Hussein could survive after such overwhelming defeats, and if so, whether Iran would invade Iraq. Iraq's financial reserves were virtually exhausted from the prolonged effort to sustain the war. Also, Iraqi oil production was down to only 750,000 barrels per day, because in April, Syria had shut off pipelines carrying Iraqi oil through to the Mediterranean. The Gulf states, especially Saudi Arabia, were deeply concerned at the prospect of an Iranian invasion of Iraq which, if successful, would leave them virtually defenseless.

Immediately after the battle for Khorramshahr, Saudi Arabia began hectic efforts to find some way of stabilizing the situation. The Saudis "were spurred by the Iranian offensive to endorse a trip of Oman's Sultan Qabus to Egypt," in an effort to get Egyptian military intervention in the case of a complete Iraqi collapse.[69] On May 17, 1982, Egypt announced it would not send troops into Iraq, and when Iraq made further appeals to Egypt, Mubarak himself announced on May 29 that Egyptian troops would not be used to support the Iraqi regime.

---

69 ibid., p. 383.

Saudi Arabian Oil Policy and the Iran-Iraq War

The Saudis then turned to the Syrians on the assumption that they could somehow play a moderating role on Iran, and keep it from invading Iraq. For this unsure aid, the Saudis were forced to make a public statement distancing themselves from Egypt declaring that "Egypt could not return to the Arab ranks until the reasons for its isolation had disappeared."[70]

The Saudis further depended on the United States interceding to keep Iran from invading Iraq, without implicating Saudi Arabia in the process. The Saudis feared being seen as too close to the United States. This seemed to be the case when on May 21, Secretary of Defense Weinberger stated that "an Iranian military victory over Iraq was not in America's interest." Also, the United States was reported to be quietly
"seeking help from Islamic nations such as Turkey, Malaysia, Pakistan, Indonesia, and Algeria" to put pressure on Iran to seek a settlement with Iraq now that Iraq was pressed. On May 26, in a major policy address, Secretary of State Haig declared that the United states would play "a more active role" to end the conflict, and would defend its "vital interests" in the Persian Gulf if other Gulf states were threatened.[71]

Saudi Arabia continued to cooperate with OPEC in an effort to hold up the oil market by continued Saudi cuts in production. These factors, especially U.S. pressure, seemed to be having their desired effects, for after Haig's speech, Iran declared it was "not adventurous and would not seek to cut the flow of oil in the Gulf."[72] On May 29, Syrian President Assad gave assurances that Iran would not invade Iraq, and on June 4, Iran declared its terms for peace, which were stiff but left room for negotiation, and on June 10, Iraq declared a

---

70 ibid., p. 383.
71 ibid., pp. 383-384.
72 ibid., p. 384.

unilateral ceasefire, and promised to withdraw to the border within two weeks.

These hopes came crashing down around the Saudis and the Iraqis when on June 21, Ayatollah Khomeyni rejected all the terms of the settlement then under discussion. On July 14, 1982, Iranian armies entered Iraq and began a powerful drive towards Basra.

The Aftermath

From late 1981 Saudi Arabia had continued to cut its production in support of the OPEC price. At the July 1982 OPEC minister's meeting in Vienna, Iran, imposing after its dramatic victories over Iraq, accused Saudi Arabia of having too great a percentage of OPEC production, and suggested that Saudi Arabia's quota should go down further to 5 mbd, and Iran's should go up. The other members of OPEC followed the Iranian example, and attacked Saudi Arabia in order to increase their own quotas. With nothing to fall back on, Saudi Arabia was forced to make further reductions in its production, so that by August, Saudi Arabia was only producing 5.5 mbd.

Just as in 1979 Saudi Arabia was forced to abandon its stated position out of short-term political pressure precipitated by a drastic shift in the regional balance of power. In 1979, it was the fall of the Shah which allowed Iraq and Syria to isolate Egypt, and to intimidate Saudi Arabia for their own particular reasons. Then, Saudi Arabia was forced to ostracize Egypt, and cut its production to facilitate a price hike. In 1982, it was a series of crushing defeats dealt to Iraq by Iran that changed the perceived balance of power, at least temporarily. This time Saudi Arabia was forced to cut its production in half over a six month period (from October 1981 to March 1982) in order to to defend OPEC pricing, and again, it was forced to accept the political agenda of the radicals.

It seemed for a while that Iran would be able to overrun Iraq, but even if that failed to come about, Iran's position and leverage was greatly enhanced along with that of its allies, Syria and the Steadfastness Block. Saudi Arabia was again surrounded by dangerous radicals who dominated Middle East politics and OPEC pricing policy.

Unlike 1979 though, world oil demand had changed dramatically, along with oil supplies. The West no longer consumed as much oil as it had at one time, and there were numerous non-OPEC supplies being developed. In fact:

> The seven leading OECD countries cut oil use in their economies as a whole by 3.2% in 1973-1976 period, but the cut was a dramatic 23.4% in 1978-81 for an accumulative drop of 27.6% from 1973.[73]

Furthermore:

> OPEC crude oil production in 1981 suffered a drop of 4.4 mbd to 22.5 mbd, and non-OPEC Free World rose 3.2% to 18.9 mbd.[74]

The consumers of the world were simply less dependent on OPEC oil. The effect of Saudi cuts in 1981 and 1982 did not boost oil prices as the OPEC radicals hoped, but it did begin a damaging drain of Saudi reserves. It also demonstrated how fragile Saudi Arabian oil policy is when pitted against the radical political forces of the Middle East.

---

73 Petroleum Intelligence Weekly, January 25, 1982.
74 Petroleum Intelligence Weekly, February 22, 1982.

Chapter 5: Saudi Arabian Oil Policy – Summer of 1982 to 1985

Overview

By March 1982, it was obvious that OPEC's ability to set world oil prices had slipped dramatically. Spot prices were falling due to Saudi Arabia's high production levels during 1980 to late 1981, but, more importantly, due to a general lowering of expected demand for OPEC oil. The West was successfully increasing its conservation efforts and its exploration and recovery of oil, so that its reliance upon OPEC oil as a fuel was steadily declining. This posed a severe challenge for the OPEC radicals who desired higher prices.

Following the summer of 1982, OPEC suffers a continual loss of its share of the international oil market, with resulting efforts to prop up its sagging price structure. OPEC's main instrument in the effort to support its price was Saudi Arabia. The OPEC radicals depended upon Saudi Arabia cutting its production in the face of an ever-decreasing demand for OPEC oil.

The fact that this action went against Saudi Arabia's fundamental economic and political interests meant that political pressure would have to be brought to bear against Saudi Arabia in order to obtain Saudi cooperation. Iran's failure to defeat Iraq in July 1982 lessened the threat to the Saudis, but did not remove it. Iraq's surprising resistance lessened the danger of an Iranian victory, but did not reverse the momentum Iran had accumulated within OPEC.

In March 1983, at the OPEC meeting in London, OPEC agreed to a price reduction in its marker crude. Though this action was more in line with Saudi interests in price moderation, it did not represent a victory for Saudi Arabia and the OPEC conservatives. The reduction was simply a reaction to the reality of the international oil market. Saudi Arabia was still left to take the brunt of the production cuts for OPEC prices, though reduced, were still at too high a level for the market to absorb. Until the summer or 1985, Iranian pressure on Saudi Arabia in large measure achieved its goals of forcing Saudi Arabia to absorb OPEC cuts in production to maintain a relatively high price.

The Role of the Radicals and Saudi Arabia

Though the OPEC radicals could not alter the West's decreasing demand for OPEC oil (at least not in the short-term), the radicals used OPEC as a forum to pressure Saudi Arabia to lower its production and absorb the necessary production cuts, rather than cut OPEC's price and thus distribute the loss more evenly. After Iraq's military defeats in the first half of 1982, and Iran's subsequent increase in influence, Saudi Arabia was particularly susceptible to such pressure.

During the next three yeas Saudi Arabia seemed to lead the effort to defend OPEC prices by severely cutting its own production, despite the serious disadvantages that this posed for Saudi Arabia. This is because Saudi Arabia's role of "swing producer" entailed unilaterally cutting its production in the face of a weak market so that the rest of OPEC could produce at their stated quotas. The Saudis acted as "swing producer" due to Iranian pressure rather than for any economic purposes. The policies that Saudi Arabia supported during this period were decidedly against their short-term economic interests, as well as their long-term political interests, but served to appease threats.

Indeed, in 1982, Saudi Arabia deficit spent slightly in order to meet its budget needs, but by 1983, the gap between Saudi expenditures and its revenues grew dramatically. In 1983, the annual deficit was $16.3 billion, in 1984, it came to $24 billion, and by 1985, the annual deficit was $25 billion, with no relief in sight.[75] Saudi Arabia covered these deficits by drawing from its reserves. But at this rate, it would be only four or five more years before Saudi Arabia would deplete its financial resources completely. In essence, Saudi Arabia was incurring the heavy costs of OPEC's oil policy, and other nations producing at higher rates were receiving all the benefits.

What was of even greater concern for the Saudis was the long-term effects of these policies. The Saudi concern in the 1970s that increased prices would spur the West to greater conservation and exploration, and in turn cause Saudi Arabia to lose its share of the market, had proven to be true. Continuing such a policy of high prices and low production could only exacerbate the problem, and possibly result in the permanent change in Western energy dependence away f om oil in general. This would be a long-term disaster for Saudi Arabia, whose tremendous oil reserves made it keenly interested in protecting its market share, not just for the next few years, but for the next hundred years. Thus it is significant that from 1982 to 1985, Saudi Arabia chose to cut

---

75 Middle East Economic Digest, December 21, 1985.

its production in support of a disagreeable OPEC policy, despite the extreme economic costs it would have to incur.

The Gulf and the Iran-Iraq War from March 1982 to January 1983

As stated before, Iran's victories over Iraq in late 1981 and early 1982 put severe pressure on Saudi Arabia and the other Gulf conservatives. In this period Iran began to drive Iraqi forces out of its territory and across the international border. The weaker sheikdoms of the U.A.E. were the first to show signs of conciliation towards Iran, whose position was greatly enhanced due to the war. Iran in return tried to woo the sheikdoms away from Saudi Arabia. This strategy was designed to further isolate Saudi Arabia from its traditional allies in the Gulf.

At the Emergency Meeting in April 20, 1982, of the Gulf Cooperation Conference (GCC) the foreign ministers adopted a neutral stance concerning the Iran-Iraq War, where only two months before they had taken a strong anti-Iranian stand.[76] Held right after the shattering March offensive by Iran, and a week before the start of a further Iranian offensive on April 29, this meeting of the GCC reflected the deep-seated fear that the GCC representatives felt in regard to Iran.

The increased position of power and influence held by Iran in the Gulf arena translated into an equally powerful and influential role within OPEC. With Iran's success against Iraq, OPEC's agenda came more and more to reflect Iran's own demands concerning oil politics. Iran's goals were to increase its own production at the expense of Iraq and those Gulf states which had supported Iraq, mainly Saudi Arabia. Iran

---

76 Mylroie, p. 350.

wanted to maximize its revenues to pay the expenses of the war with Iraq, its highest priority. In the months that followed the Iranian victories against Iraq, there was a steady increase in Iranian oil production, and a precipitous decrease in Iraqi and Saudi oil productions.

In April 1983, Iraq's oil production was reduced by 400,000 barrels per day to a low of 800,000 barrels per day by Syria's cut-off of Iraq's East Mediterranean pipeline.[77] Following this cut-off, Iran started an intense drive to capture Iraq's clients in order to increase its exports. By June, this strategy had proven to be very successful. Iranian production for June and July was up over a million barrels per day, (a 100% increase) from 1.1 mbd in March to 2.2 mbd.[78] More significantly though, in July, Iran successfully signed a host of long-term contracts with the major Japanese oil companies, signaling a major coup for Iran:

> Iran initially faced rough going as it tried to sell to Japan, but its cut-rate prices – **plus its success in the war** – eventually prompted eleven Japanese companies to sign nine- to twelve-month contracts.[79]

In sharp contrast, Iraq and Saudi Arabia failed to keep their customers, or to maintain their production. Clearly, Iran's military victories in 1982 had translated into direct political and economic gains, recognized worldwide.

For Saudi Arabia, the reduction in its production was due to more subtle pressure than having its pipelines closed down. Since Saudi Arabia unlike Iraq, had unrestrained access to the

---
77 Petroleum Intelligence Weekly, April 19, 1982.
78 Petroleum Intelligence Weekly derived figures.
79 Petroleum Intelligence Weekly, July 5, 1982.

Saudi Arabian Oil Policy and the Iran-Iraq War

ocean it was in some respects more independent in its ability to produce and ship its oil than Iraq, but in many other more significant ways Saudi Arabia was vulnerable. With long borders and an inadequate defense, Saudi Arabia depends upon promoting a balance among its neighboring Arab states to enable it to pursue its policies. This held especially true within OPEC. With support for its policies of high production and price moderation virtually non-existent within OPEC, Saudi Arabia allowed Iran to dictate Saudi production cuts.

In January 1982, Saudi Arabia allowed its production to fall from 8.5 mbd to 7.5 mbd in the face of weak world wide demand. While other OPEC members, Iran foremost among them, were offering significant discounts for their oil, Saudi Arabia held to the $34 OPEC price, which was virtually unsellable.[80] At the March OPEC meeting in Vienna, Saudi Arabia accepted a further cut, this time in the form of an actual production ceiling, down to 7.0 mbd.[81] These production cuts were made in the face of extreme long-term and short-term costs which must have been known to the Saudis. In March, Petroleum Intelligence Weekly reported of a new forecast which declared that Saudi Arabia needed at least 8 mbd in oil production to cover the cost of its five year plan:

> Anything more than a short-term cutback in oil production would be counter-productive to the Kingdom's interest... A short-term cutback to, say, 6.2 mbd, would not pose unmanageable problems in the short-term,... but holding production to that level for an entire year could result in an annual Saudi deficit of $31-billion.[82]

---

80 Petroleum Intelligence Weekly, February 23, 1982.
81 New York Times, March 21, 1982.
82 Petroleum Intelligence Weekly, March 1, 1982.

Saudi Arabian Oil Policy and the Iran-Iraq War

Saudi Arabia may have felt that any cuts it would make due to Iranian pressure would only be short-term, but this was not in fact likely and if so it would have been a major miscalculation. Iranian pressure on Saudi Arabia was a result of Iranian success in the war and its newly concluded alliance with Syria, and there was no relief in sight. By the end of the spring of 1982, Saudi Arabia must have realized better than anyone that Iran was in a dominant position in the Gulf and in OPEC. With Iraq seemingly on the point of collapse, Iranian benevolence seemed to be the only hope for the weaker Gulf states. Only a turn-around in the war would change this situation, and that seemed unlikely.

Still, hope combined with delaying tactics are some of the few policy avenues that the weak can pursue and this was what the Saudis appeared to be doing at this stage:

> With no option in sight but to explore Iran's good will and hope for a reversal of Iraq's (poor) fortunes, a modicum of relief came from an entirely unexpected quarter. As Iran readied its invasion of Iraq, Israel invaded Lebanon on June 6.[83]

The Israeli invasion of Lebanon initially raised Saudi and Iraqi hopes of a settlement of the Iran-Iraq War, but ended a month later in Iran's utter refusal to negotiate.

In weakening Syrian influence in Arab politics, if only temporarily, the Israeli invasion of Lebanon gave Saudi Arabia more leverage over Syria in that Syria needed Saudi Arabia's access to the United States. The invasion further relieved pressure on Iraq, which had to deploy troops on its Western border against Syria, lessening its ability to defend

---

83 Mylroie, p. 353.

against Iran. Furthermore, Saudi Arabia and Iraq hoped for a possible settlement of the Iran-Iraq War based on a call for Islamic unity in the wake of Israel's invasion of Lebanon.

Iran had set stiff terms, but had left room for negotiations, and Iraq's declaration of a unilateral ceasefire on June 10, and withdrawal in response to the Israeli invasion of Lebanon further encouraged this hope. Saudi oil production in this atmosphere went back up to 6.5 mbd during the month of June, taking advantage of a slight increase in market demand, showing increased confidence on the part of the Saudis.

This period of about two weeks proved to be the exception rather than the rule for Saudi oil policy in 1982. By mid-June, Iran had increased its claims for reparations to $150 billion, and was taking a hard-line against the moderate Gulf states, especially Saudi Arabia, sending out calls for the overthrow of the Kingdom over the radio.[84] On June 21, Ayatollah Khomeyni rejected all the terms then under discussion, and it became obvious that nothing would stop the Iranian invasion of Iraq.

The Invasion of Iraq

The long awaited Iranian invasion of Iraq began on July 14, 1982, in an offensive called Operation Ramadan. At first the Iranians were very successful, utilizing the by now standard tactic of human waves of Revolutionary Guards to clear out the minefields and trench fortifications, followed by more conventional forces. The Iraqis were pushed back some ten to twenty-five kilometers.[85] As the Iranians began entering the marshes north of Basra, they began to run into stiff resistance.

---

84 Petroleum Intelligence Weekly, June 14, 1982.
85 MECS, 1981-82, p. 313.

Saudi Arabian Oil Policy and the Iran-Iraq War

Then Iraq counter-attacked pushing Iranian troops back almost to the frontier.

The strength of Iraq's resistance was surprising and gave a certain amount of relief to the Saudis and allowed them to slowly try to rebuild a more moderate consensus in the Gulf:

> Had Iran succeeded in invading and defeating Iraq, it would have dominated the Gulf. Only the unanticipated strength of Iraqi resistance on home ground saved the situation. Chastened by Iran's near success, in the protracted stalemate that followed the failure of the Iranian invasion of Iraq, Riyadh led the shaykdoms (slowly) in coordinating their defenses, as Riyadh regained the chance to establish its dominance on the Arab littoral relatively unhindered by the Gulf's Big Two.[86]

With Syria temporarily removed by Israel's invasion of Lebanon, and Iraq's position now stabilized, the threat was less direct but still present. Saudi Arabian oil production continued to fall in response to Iranian pressure in OPEC. World demand for oil was falling, and non-OPEC sources were increasing their share of the market. Though unsuccessful in toppling Iraq, Iran was very successful within OPEC. From August to the end of the 1982, Saudi Arabian oil production hovered at 5.5 mbd, and Iranian rose from 2.1 mbd to 2.8 mbd.[87]

In August 1982, the Iraqis extended the conflict into the Gulf region with an air offensive by declaring an "exclusion zone" in which shipping intended for Iran would be attacked by the Iraqi air force. Further, Iraq began more intensive attacks

---

86 Mylroie, p. 350.
87 Petroleum Intelligence Weekly derived figures.

against Iranian installations; these attacks "consisted mainly in aerial bombing of Iranian tankers, the port of Bandar Khomeyni, and the oil terminal on Kharg Island.[88] This offensive was targeted at destroying Iranian oil commerce, and thus destroy its ability to wage war against Iraq. This was a strategy well suited to the Iraqis for they had long lost their ability to export from the Gulf, and could thus attack with virtual impunity. Unfortunately, Iraq simply did not have the requisite naval or air forces to do any real damage. Not until 1984 did Iraqi threats begin to take the shape of effective attacks.·

Saudi Arabian Oil Policy from 1983 to 1985

During this period, the demand for OPEC oil steadily dropped as the West became less dependent on oil in general, and OPEC oil in particular. In fact, the OPEC hope that a world wide economic recovery would increase demand for oil seemed dubious at best. Studies showed that oil use was falling regardless of whether Western economies were expanding or contracting. In fact it seemed that economic recovery often went to funding newer, more efficient, conservation and substitution efforts.[89] OPEC had simply priced itself out of the market.

Despite the economic reality of these facts, the political reality within OPEC allowed for very little downward movement in prices. As long as the radicals led by Iran held sway within OPEC, price reductions would be limited. At the beginning of 1983, prices were lowered somewhat, but after that all efforts to stabilize the market were done with production quotas which were aimed at cutting OPEC

---

88 MECS, 1981-82, p. 313.
89 Petroleum Intelligence Weekly, July 5, 1982.

production by unilateral cuts in Saudi Arabian production. Saudi Arabia's reaction to a steadily falling market was to slowly try to build a consensus, and wait for an opportune moment to act.

The London Agreement

In January 1983, at the OPEC meeting in Geneva, OPEC failed to reach an agreement on price and production levels. Saudi Arabia wanted other members to discontinue offering large discounts before it would accept the proposed 17.5 mbd production ceiling. Nigeria, Algeria, Libya, and Iran all discounted their oil three to four dollars a barrel from the $34 OPEC marker crude. After the unsuccessful meeting, Sheikh Yamani threatened to lower Saudi crude prices as well.[90] By January, Saudi production had fallen to 4.6 mbd, whereas Iranian production had held at 2.7 mbd.

In February of 1983, Saudi Arabia and five other OPEC nations decided to lower prices of their Arabian Light Crude to $30 per barrel, a $4 cut in price. This was a response to numerous acts of price cutting by other OPEC nations, especially Nigeria which had lowered its price $5.50 per barrel in response to lowered North Sea oil prices.[91] This action by Saudi Arabia can not be viewed as an effort to undercut the market price, for it was not accompanied by an increase in Saudi production. In fact Saudi production fell further to 3.6 mbd from 4.6 mbd in January. The Saudi action was a hesitant response to what had become an unmanageable situation. OPEC simply could not support a $34 price structure regardless of how much Saudi Arabia reduced its production.

---

90 New York Times, January, 25, 1983.
91 New York Times, February 24, 1983.

Saudi Arabian Oil Policy and the Iran-Iraq War

In March, OPEC met in London, and lowered the official price to $29 per barrel, and set a new production ceiling of 17.5 mbd, though this ceiling was actually a million barrels over what OPEC was at that time producing. The truly significant development that came out of the Long Agreement was the formal adoption by Saudi Arabia of the responsibility as "swing producer." As Robert Hershey stated in his analysis of the OPEC meeting:

> Not only has Saudi Arabia's production quota been cut from 7 million barrels a day to a maximum of 5 million, they alone are charged with lowering it if demand drops in order to let other members continue producing at their allotted quotas.[92]

Thus, the ceiling of 17.5 mbd only meant that if OPEC production needed to go below this level in order to hold up the price, Saudi Arabia would have to provide all of the cuts.

As A. M. El-Mokadem points out, the London Agreement had three major faults. Foremost among these was the fact that even with the price cut to $29 per barrel, the discounted price at this time was at $26.40 per barrel:

> Secondly, the Agreement appears to be very fragile. It assumes that it is acceptable to the non-OPEC producers in general, whereas only Mexico showed a significant degree of 'understanding.' In particular, it is conditional on Britain not reducing the price of North Sea Oil below its present level of $30.20 (Forties) and on the Iranians taking advantage of the special allowances made to them in a responsible way. The latter cannot be guaranteed at a time of war. Thirdly, no deterrent is

---

92 Robert D. Hershey, "Accord Called Evidence of Limit to Saudi Power,"

envisaged other than the fear of the collapse of OPEC and the theoretical leadership of the Saudis.[93]

The ultimate result of the March meeting was that for the next two years, Saudi Arabia acted as the "swing producer," much to its economic and political disadvantage. Indeed, low production and high prices caused long-term harm to Saudi economic interests, and it also strengthened Iran. Since Iran was able to produce at only a limited level, any increase in price meant more money for its war effort, and thus more instability in the Gulf and for Saudi Arabia. In order to prop up an OPEC price that did not really give any real benefit, Saudi Arabia was further forced to deficit spend dramatically to cover its considerable expenditures.

Yet, even assuming Saudi willingness to act as swing producer, and the cut in price to $29 per barrel, demand for OPEC oil failed to pick-up, though some spot prices began to near the OPEC level. In April, the Petroleum Intelligence Weekly noted, "OPEC's crude oil production still drooping at around 14 mbd 5 weeks after the groups 15% price rollbacks."[94] Also, even in April signs of Saudi unwillingness, or inability, to meet the responsibilities of a "swing producer" were apparent. In later April, Saudi production began to move up slightly from its low of 3 mbd up to around 4 mbd: "As swing producer, Saudi Arabia should (have kept) its production at 3 mbd until all others reach(ed) their quotas."[95]

The Renewed Stalemate 1983

---

93 El-Mokadem, p. 44.
94 Petroleum Intelligence Weekly, April 18, 1983.
95 Petroleum Intelligence Weekly, April 25, 1983.

Saudi Arabian Oil Policy and the Iran-Iraq War

The third year of the war remained characterized by the initiative on the ground held by the Iranians, relying on the grand tactic of the big break through, using human waves to make up for deficiencies in equipment. Iraq continued to carry the conflict into the Gulf by maintaining an "exclusion zone." This zone was only laxly enforced due to Iraq's insufficient military forces, and political pressure from the Gulf states which feared Iranian reprisals against their shipping.

The war aims of the belligerents remained basically the same. Iran provided unflinching rejection of all peace plans that did not contain condemnation and punishment for the regime of Saddam Hussein, and Iraq was desperately seeking some way out of the war which it had started. As group after group went to Iran with proposals for settlement of the war, Iran's response was invariably to the effect that the proposals "contained nothing new and raised points which Iran had previously rejected."[96] Iran's stance seemed to be summed up in words attributed to Ayatollah Khomeyni:

> There are no conditions. The only condition is that the regime in Baghdad must fall, and must be replaced by an Islamic Republic chosen by the Muslim people in the land between the two rivers.[97]

With this in mind, on February 6, 1983, Iran launched its greatest offensive of the war up to that point: "Val Fajr" or "before sunrise." With a force of six divisions, the Iranians hoped to capture the Basra-Baghdad road, and drive a wedge between the main Iraqi forces on the front and the capital. The Iranians failed in their initial attempt, and on April 10, tried

---

96 MECS, 1982-83, p. 258.
97 MECS, 1982-83, p. 259.

again with the same results. The Iranian casualties were reported by Iraq to be 15,000 dead. This offensive which Rafsanjani had originally claimed "was the final move towards ending the war," was halted, according to Rafsanjani, because of "Iranian interest to spare enemy soldiers who were to serve the future Islamic Republic of Iraq."[98]

The next Iranian offensive came in the northern sector on July 22, 1983, and was called "Val Fajr II." The Iranians hoped to put pressure on the oil producing Kirkuk province, and to encourage Iraqi Kurds to rebel against Baghdad, but their efforts proved inconclusive. In August further attacks ware carried out in the northern sector by Iran, but with no real results.

The Iraqis launched a limited offensive against the south-central sector in August which was quickly halted and repelled. The real Iraqi initiative remained in its actions in the Gulf. Though Iraq lacked the naval and air forces to properly enforce their "exclusion zone" and shut down Iranian facilities, Iraqi activities triggered a drop in Iranian oil exports to a limited extent, and occasionally delivered damaging attacks to Iranian oil facilities. This was reflected in the Iranian threats in August to block the Gulf if Iraq crippled its oil exporting ability.[99]

The stalemate on the ground and the Iraqi attacks on Iranian oil exports allowed Saudi Arabia, as 1983 progressed, to begin timid efforts to regain its influence by increasing support for Iraq. In July, Saudi Arabia and Kuwait both used their Neutral Zone production to help pay Iraqi war debts: "Saudi Arabia is reportedly ready to earmark up to a

---

98   ibid., p. 256.
99   Petroleum Intelligence Weekly, August 1, 1983.

maximum of 200,000 bd in 'war relief' oil aid for Iraq."[100] By November, oil aid to Iraq exceeded this limit and reached a 300,000 bd level.[101] Furthermore, Iraq and Saudi Arabia agreed to build a pipeline to the Red Sea that would carry .500 mbd of Iraqi crude by mid 1985.[102]

In November, Iran began pressing for a $5 increase in OPEC prices with the argument that the London Agreement's $5 decrease in price had failed to revive demand.[103] Though these suggestions were rejected in the December OPEC meeting in Geneva, an agreement was reached only when Iran agreed to drop its demands for a $5 increase, and Saudi Arabia "reluctantly reaffirmed its role as group's swing producer, agreeing to raise and lower production according to world demand."[104] By the end of 1983, Saudi Arabia was still in the uncomfortable position of "swing producer" providing reluctant support for radical demands.

The Gulf Dimension 1984

As the war continued into what seemed to be an endless stream of brutal, useless offensives, the Gulf level of the conflict became much more important, especially given the strategic importance of the Gulf to Iran and the other Gulf states, and its relative unimportance to Iraq. The expansion of the war into the Gulf high-lighted the weaknesses of both Saudi Arabia to defend itself against Iran, and Iran to effectively control the situation in the Persian Gulf. It also led to a surprising increase in OPEC production that worsened

---

100 Petroleum Intelligence Weekly, July 11, 1983.
101 Petroleum Intelligence Weekly, November 21, 1983.
102 Petroleum Intelligence Weekly, November 28, 1983.
103 New York Times, November 17, 1983.
104 New York Times, December 9, 1983.

the already difficult position of the price hawks to maintain high prices.

In April and May of 1984, Iraq began an intensive series of attacks against tankers entering Iranian ports. Intensification of the Gulf spectrum of the war gave Iraq many advantages in that it "provide(d) some of the strategic depth Iraq lacks in the battlefield, draws the Gulf states into active support, and forces the Western powers also to become more involved."[105]

During this period, Iranian oil exports at one point dropped to an all time low of 500,000 to 600,000 barrels a day from a previous wartime average of about 2 million barrels a day. Though the drop was artificially steep, due more to Iran's failure to immediately offer discounts to compensate for the increase in insurance rates for ships bound for Iran than to any actual damage inflicted by Iraq, the experience "must be sobering for Teheran's leaders to ponder."[106] Such levels of production would make it very difficult, possibly even impossible, for the Iranians to continue the war effort.

Virtually the only way Iran could counter the Iraqi war in the Gulf was to attack the other Gulf states' shipping and facilities. This would have been a very dangerous proposition for Iran for it could bring the Western powers into the war in a united front against Iran. The Saudi reaction to this threat was to begin developing a "floating storage" of close to 55 million barrels. In January 1984, Saudi Arabia began building up a flotilla of large tankers filled with oil hanging off the destination ports of the world, but not up for sale.[107] These were a strategic reserve that Saudi Arabia was developing to

---

105 Michael Sterner, "The Iran-Iraq War," Foreign Affairs, Fall 1984, vol. 63, no. 1, p. 133.
106 ibid., p. 134.
107 Petroleum Intelligence Weekly, January 9 and 23, 1984.

Saudi Arabian Oil Policy and the Iran-Iraq War

blunt any Iranian attacks against it and to generally give Saudi Arabia a more flexible response to any threats that may be posed against it:

> Many political analysts and oil market specialist are convinced (that) the primary motivation now is to obtain emergency protection from a Mideast political explosion. A big new Iraqi offensive would probably prompt Iran to try and block the Straits of Hormuz or knock out Saudi oil export terminals – a compelling reason for Riyadh to put an oil supply safety net outside the region.[108]

Further deterrence to Iran existed in the fact that closing the Straits of Hormuz would hurt Iran as much, or more, than it would hurt the other Gulf states:

> A total cessation of exports through the Gulf by Iran, Kuwait, and Saudi Arabia – amounting to some 6 to 6.5 million b/d – could be made up by other exporters and use of the U.S. strategic stockpile.[109]

In the end the combined threat of Western intervention and Saudi Arabia's stockpiling of crude prevented any retaliatory strikes from Iran. The ultimate result of the whole affair, in fact, turned out to be exactly the opposite of what everyone had feared:

> Apart from very brief disruptions, tanker tactics by warring Iran and Iraq did more to add to Mideast oil supplies in the second quarter than reduce them, as exporters and oil buyers compensated for

---
108 Petroleum Intelligence Weekly, January 23, 1984.
109 Petroleum Intelligence Weekly, June 4. 1984.

cut offs that never materialized. The resulting confusion complicated OPEC's already difficult task of monitoring members' actual output levels.[110]

Though 72 vessels were attacked during the year 1984 by both Iran and Iraq, there was little actual negative effect on the market accept in very sporadic events.[111]

As the year progressed, fears of an OPEC price war began to surface. In October 1984, OPEC met in Geneva to try to avert this price war, and to prop up weakening oil prices. OPEC reached an agreement declaring an across the board cutback of 8+%, but countries that wanted to overproduce could do so if they found another OPEC country to carry their quota cuts. This other country was inevitably Saudi Arabia, and the resulting cuts again fell heavily upon the Saudis who had to make cutbacks of 647,000 bd.[112] From a summer high of 5.25 mbd, Saudi production fell to 3.8 mbd for November.[113]

By December 1984, oil prices continued to fall even though winter traditionally supplied an upturn for the market. Saudi production cuts had brought its production down to 3.4 mbd.[114] The market could not support the OPEC pricing structure and discounting within OPEC was rampant. Though Saudi Arabia was faithfully fulfilling its role as "swing producer" prices continued to fall. By early 1985, OPEC seemed to be falling apart, with Subruto of Indonesia claiming that, "Theoretically, there is no marker anymore.

---

110 Petroleum Intelligence Weekly, July 16, 1984.
111 Middle East Economic Digest, September 13-19, 1986.
112 New York Times, March 15, 1984.
113 Petroleum Intelligence Weekly derived Figures.
114 Petroleum Intelligence Weekly derived Figures.

Saudi Arabian Oil Policy and the Iran-Iraq War

The fundamentals of the market will determine the price of oil."[115]

The 1985 Deterioration of OPEC

In the early part of 1985, an exceptionally easy winter for the industrialized world meant that oil demand was down, and OPEC again felt the pinch. By June, Saudi Arabia, which was still serving as the "swing producer," was producing only 2.5 mbd, a level that the Saudis said could not be sustained for long periods of time without creating serious economic and structural problems. By late summer, Saudi Arabia's oil production actually fell to below 2 mbd. Continued use of discounts and price slashing by producers made the price structure untenable. In July 1985, OPEC proposed to cut prices $1.00 to 1.50 per barrel but no measure was agreed upon due to radical opposition. By August, Saudi Arabia seemed to have abandoned its position as "swing producer," and threatened to produce 4 mbd.

---

[115] New York Time, January 31, 1985.

Chapter 6: The Price War – August 1985 to December 1986

Overview

From August 1985 to August 1986, Saudi Arabia pursued what must be termed a "price war." Economically pressed, Saudi Arabia took advantage of Iran's relative weakness in the Gulf and in OPEC to begin increasing its production dramatically in an effort to recapture its long-term share of the market. At the December OPEC meeting the Saudi agenda dominated the proceedings. By the summer of 1986, the spot price of oil had fallen to a low of $9 a barrel, posing serious economic difficulties for many OPEC countries, but especially Iran, which was also facing serious problems in actually exporting its oil. This turn of events not only allowed Saudi Arabia to pursue a long-term economic policy that was more in its interest, but also allowed it in the same stroke to follow a political policy that isolated and weakened Iran, a serious threat to Saudi security interests. But in August of 1986, Saudi Arabia suddenly abandoned its price war, and relinquished its role of policy leader within OPEC back to Iran.

The End of the Swing Producer

After three disastrous years as swing producer, Saudi Arabia made another about-face change in oil policy. Saudi Arabia's economy was hurting after three years of cutting its production to support OPEC's price. Due to declining

Saudi Arabian Oil Policy and the Iran-Iraq War

revenues and the increased cost of Iraqi war aid, the slump in the Saudi economy was having severe effects on Saudi Arabia's private sector as well. In 1984, 1500 Saudi owned companies folded or had need of emergency financing, and the gross domestic product for Saudi Arabia was 40% to 50% down from what it previously had been.[116]

Even the financial power of Saudi Arabia was beginning to be questioned when it began having difficulties paying its bills to U.S. banks and companies. Saudi Arabian deficit spending, which for the last few years had been draining the Saudi coffers, seemed to be reaching a new high. The 1984 budget deficit was $24 billion, but 1985 was expected to be even worse.[117] The Director of the Middle East Services at Wharton Econometrics said in February 1985:

> Right now, the Saudis are at a juncture in which the entire economy is changing gears from a construction-based growth economy into a much more sober, production-based economy. All of the investments made in industry, infrastructure and the like now have to start paying off.[118]

Indeed, something had to start "paying off," for Saudi Arabia had reached the breaking point financially. Saudi Arabia needed to produce 4 mbd, which translates into $35 billion per year, for revenue stability. By the summer of 1985, with only 2 mbd in production, Saudi Arabia needed money.
Business Week stated:

---

116 Kenneth N. Gilpin, "Saudi Economy is Ailing," New York Times, February 18, 1985.
117 Middle East Economic Digest, December 21 1985. p. 76.
118 Gilpin.

Saudi Arabian Oil Policy and the Iran-Iraq War

The need to retain that financial influence, vital to the Kingdom's security, is a major factor in King Fahd's decision to boost Saudi production instead of holding it down in a vain attempt to shore up OPEC's oil-price structure.[119]

These economic factors, though they had always been present, began to be felt ever more strongly in Saudi Arabia. The economic pressures, plus a politically opportune atmosphere, allowed Saudi Arabia to break with OPEC, abandon its role as swing producer, and begin efforts to reestablish its dominance in the world oil market.

A major aspect of Saudi Arabia's ability to take the lead within OPEC was a perceived change in the Iran-Iraq War. In August 1985, Iraq launched a series of determined attacks against the Iranian oil loading facilities of Kharg Island. On August 15, Iraq began aerial attacks against Kharg dedicated to the destruction of the oil terminal:

> Marine salvage executives on (the) Persian Gulf say that Iraqi jets inflicted enormous damage on Iran's vast Kharg Island oil terminal, but that two of its three loading Jetties may still be operating.[120]

Throughout September, October, November, and December, Iraq kept up a steady stream of attacks against Kharg until by December 30, Iran declared that it had abandoned the island as a facility for the loading of oil.[121]

---

119 John Pearson, ed., "The Saudies Had to Pump More Oil or lose Mideast Influence," Business Week, December 30, 1985, p. 65.
120 New York Times, August 17, 1985.
121 New York Times, December 30, 1985.

Saudi Arabian Oil Policy and the Iran-Iraq War

These attacks seriously reduced Iran's oil exports, at a time when Iraqi exports were increasing due to the construction of numerous pipelines. What is also significant is that Saudi Arabia at this point began to raise its production in a decision which eventually drove down the price of oil dramatically. The Saudi actions, when viewed along side the Iraqi disabling of Kharg, suggests that Iraq and Saudi Arabia may have been trying to force Iran into a settlement through depriving it of its oil revenue.

Iraq's determined resistance on the ground in facing offensive after offensive, in the Gulf with its elimination of Kharg, and in its numerous attacks against Iranian bound shipping, even in the face of serious concerns and objections by Iraq's Gulf neighbors, seemed to reflect the renewed vigor of Iraq in the face of Iran's continued belligerence.

The political factors that allowed Saudi Arabia to begin what in essence turned into an OPEC price war can be summed up in three parts: first, an increased confidence in the Iraqi ability to hold its own against Iranian attacks, and to cause Iran heavy costs in men, machines, and oil production; secondly, the completion of pipelines to carry increased Iraqi production, which gave Iraq a greater measure of independence; and thirdly, a general consensus within OPEC that something drastic must be done to stem the ever declining demand for OPEC oil. These factors had been developing slowly, but only in 1985 did they become strong enough to give Saudi Arabia the support it felt it needed to start a price war that would be very damaging to Saudi Arabia's major adversary in OPEC; Iran.

Saudi Arabian Oil Policy and the Iran-Iraq War

The Price War

At the beginning of August 1985, Saudi Arabia declared its intentions of lifting its production up to its OPEC quota of 4.4 mbd.[122] By the end of August though, Saudi production had actually fallen to 2.2 to 2.4 mbd despite Saudi Arabia's desire to raise it.[123] By September 1985, Saudi Arabia agreed to link its oil sales to the market price of refined products derived from it, thus insuring the buyer a profit, and the seller a client.[124] This system of sales was called netbacking, and was not an entirely new strategy for oil exporters. Iran had been selling its oil in this fashion all throughout 1985. What was new was that the Saudis abandoned their role as swing producer. Instead of supporting an OPEC price which had allowed Iran to overproduce and undersell others within OPEC, Saudi Arabia adopted a confrontational stand, increasing its production in September up to 3 mbd, and in October up 4 mbd.[125] Saudi Arabia was beginning to flood the market. By November, a Saudi Arabian national oil company official was quoted as saying that Saudi Arabia was:

> no longer willing to bear the burden of being (OPEC's) swing producer; production, at least for a time will be close to its quota of 4.3 mbd.[126]

In the December 1985 meeting of OPEC, the group decided that it must recapture a "fair share of the market," reflecting Saudi Arabia's own views, and thus Saudi Arabia's newly asserted leadership within OPEC. OPEC agreed to abandon its marker price of $28 a barrel, and accepted a new

---
122 New York Times, August 1, 1985.
123 New York Times, August 26, 1985.
124 New York Times, September 4. 1985.
125 New York Times, October 22, 1985.
126 Middle East Economic Digest, November 9, 1985.

marketing strategy "that could lead to a new oil-price war and bring lower world prices in 1986."[127] Saudi actions led to a declared increase in volumes in December and also a drop in prices. "The Kingdom is hoping that a decline in prices will help to ensure that oil remains a primary energy source."[128]

As stated by Henry S. Rowen, the Saudis had four major economic goals in pursuing this course of action:

1. Making world oil demand grow faster.

2. Driving current high-cost production from the market.

3. Discouraging new oil investment by presenting to investors an oil market with lower and more volatile prices.

4. Shocking other oil exporters (including non-OPEC members) into sharing the burden of price maintenance through production cuts.[129]

As one analysis noted, the lowering of prices and increasing of production by the Saudis implied that the Kingdom was "embarking on a conscious effort to lower oil prices, using shock tactics to enforce discipline in an increasingly ragged and fragmented market."[130]

---

127 New York Times, December 9, 1985.
128 Middle East Economic Digest, December 14, 1985, p. 6.
129 Henry S. Rowen, "Saudi Gambit Can Succeed," Wall Street Journal, March 21, 1986.
130 Middle East Economic Digest, November 9, 1985, p. 11.

Saudi Arabian Oil Policy and the Iran-Iraq War

The Gulf War

Another aspect of the price war which was of equal if not greater importance was the political goals that the Saudis pursued by a price war:

> Two of OPEC's members, Iran and Iraq, are locked in a six-year-old war of attrition that has split the groups (OPEC) Arab members down the middle. On the one hand, moderate Sunni Muslim states along the Gulf, led by Saudi Arabia, side with Iraq, while the radical governments of North Africa, such as Libya and Algeria, throw their lot in with the revolutionary Shiite regime in Tehran.[131]

A price war offered not only an opportunity to develop a more economically rational approach to Saudi Arabian oil production, but it also weakened the radical block within OPEC which could not increase production as much as Saudi Arabia and the other Gulf states, and which therefore suffered greater revenue loss due to the drop in prices.

As an additional factor, from August of 1985 into late 1986, Iraqi attacks against Iranian oil targets began to increase in number and effectiveness. As a result of these attacks, Iranian oil exports often went below a million barrels per day, and averaged less than 1.3 mbd for 1986.[132] Indeed, Iran was forced to deal with the double jeopardy of low prices, and decreasing production.

These attacks succeeded in severely curtailing the Iranian economy by limiting its ability to get foreign exchange, and seemed to be well on the way to crippling Iran's war effort.

---

131 New York Times, August 4. 1986.
132 Middle East Economic Digest, September 27-30, 1986.

Saudi Arabian Oil Policy and the Iran-Iraq War

Starting in 1985, Iran began experiencing a serious economic downturn of drastic proportions. Iranian industrial output was down, unemployment was up, and inflation was skyrocketing:

> Between 1982-85, the annual (Iranian) growth rate peaked at 25 percent, but falling oil revenues in 1985 resulted in zero growth that year and in a sharp fall in early 1986.[133]

As the below figures indicate, the Iranian economy experienced about a 12% drop in Gross Domestic Production below pre-1982 levels due to its decreased revenues from oil.

---

[133] Middle East Economic Digest, September 27-30, 1986, p. 41.

Saudi Arabian Oil Policy and the Iran-Iraq War

Iran: Gross Domestic Product (GDP)
1981/82 – 1986/87
(IR '000 million)

81/82	82/83	83/84	84/85	85/86	86/87*
7,031.1	8,100.0	9,158.1	9,179.9	9,100.0	8,000.0

Exchange Rates:
$1 = IR 90.00 *(81/82) to (84/85)
$1 = IR 85.00 (85/86)
$1 = IR 80.00 (86/87)

Iran: Crude Oil Output
1982/83-1986/87
(Million b/d)

	82/83	83/84	84/85	85/86*	86/87*
Prod.	2,684	2,707	2,300	2,200	2,000
Exp.	2,051	2,009	1,000	1,500	1,300

* = Estimates
From (<u>Middle East Economic Digest</u>, v. 30, #39, September 27-30, 1986, p. 41)

The Iraqi successes in the Gulf, and the Saudi led price war were mutually supporting. For Saudi Arabia, Iraq's successes gave it an increased amount of leverage over others in OPEC, and for Iraq, Iran's weakened economic position inspired greater confidence in Iraq's ability to survive.

Saudi Arabian Oil Policy and the Iran-Iraq War

1986 to the End of the Price War

In January of 1986, crude oil prices fell to below $20 a barrel for the first time in six years.[134] Saudi production continued to stay at about 4 mbd. By February, oil prices had gone down to around $15 a barrel, and OPEC production had reached more than 18 mbd.[135] At the March OPEC meeting in Geneva, a confrontation occurred between those who supported the Saudi led price war, and the Iranian-North African alliance, including Algeria and Libya, which opposed the price war. It ended inconclusively when Saudi Arabia demanded that Britain must join the accord before any cuts take place.[136] Since it was obvious that Britain would not do this, the March meeting represented a victory for Saudi Arabia's ability to continue the price war despite the opposition of the radicals.

In April, crude oil prices plunged to below $10 a barrel before going back up to $14 a barrel.[137] In April, May, and June prices moved between $10 and $15 a barrel with downward pressure dominating the market. At the June OPEC meeting held in Yugoslavia, most members, including Saudi Arabia, agreed to a modest production cut to 18 mbd to stabilize prices. An agreement was not reached however, because the radicals led by Iran demanded far greater cuts in production down to 14.5 mbd in order to support a price of $28 by the end of the year.[138]

In July, due in part to increased Saudi oil production as well as the expected summer slump in energy use, crude oil prices went below $10 a barrel. Saudi production was at 5.8 mbd

---

134 New York Times, January 21, 1986.
135 New York Times, February 5, 1986.
136 New York Times, March 19, 1986.
137 New York Times, April 8, 1986.
138 New York Times, June 27, 1986.

and OPEC's total production was at 20.5 mbd.[139] Going into the Geneva OPEC meeting of late July and early August, the price war seemed to have been successful on all grounds: much Western high-cost production had been eliminated, and OPEC oil had taken its place; demand for oil in the West had picked up; and the oil companies had announced reductions in development drilling investments.[140] Furthermore, Iranian production was down along with its revenues.

Thus it came as a universal surprise when the August meeting resulted in Iran regaining OPEC leadership from Saudi Arabia, and brokering an agreement that abandoned the price war, and set in place production cuts intended to increase oil prices to around $15 to $20 a barrel.

The End of the Price War

The August 1986 OPEC meeting began with Saudi Arabia's price war coming under direct attack from OPEC radicals:

> There has been repeated charges from the Iranian camp that Saudi Arabia's tenaciously pursued policy of unrestrained production to push prices down is designed to dry up the oil revenues of Iran and cripple its war effort.[141]

Though only a month before, Saudi Arabia had been able to hold sway over the radicals, subtle changes that had been developing over a period of months broke the Saudis' temporary preeminence within OPEC. By October, Iran had virtually taken control of OPEC, as was illustrated by Saudi Arabia's removal of its long standing oil minister, Sheikh

---
139 Wall Street Journal, August 5, 1986.
140 Rowen.
141 New York Times, August 4, 1986.

Saudi Arabian Oil Policy and the Iran-Iraq War

Yamani. American arms sales to Iran, combined with a serious erosion of Saudi confidence in Iraq's ability to survive the war placed Iran in a much stronger position.

In February, Iraq lost the politically and symbolically significant port of Fao during one of Iran's most extensive offensives. Part of the Iraqi defeat was written off due to particularly unfortunate and rare weather conditions, which immobilized Iraq's heavy forces, but left Iran relatively mobile. Another explanation put forward almost immediately after the battle suggested that Iraq's defeat was due to more serious circumstances than freak weather:

> Western military analysts and diplomats say (the) Iraqi army has overwhelming superiority in firepower and equipment and almost complete mastery of air, but is being ground down by Iran because it lacks motivation and will to fight.[142]

This analysis suggested that the Iranian victory in the Fao peninsula reflected a general deterioration of Iraq's military fortitude. This argument was further strengthened in July when Iraq lost the Iranian city of Mehran which it had taken with great fan-fare in May. Though not necessarily a true evaluation, the above analysis may reflect speculations that were prevalent at the time in many high circles, American and Saudi. With this in mind, it is obvious Iran's reemergence from August to October of 1986 as the preeminent power within OPEC had been slowly developing during the previous months.

Of course there is equal danger in over-emphasizing Iranian dominance and Saudi weakness at this point. Saudi Arabia's

---

142 New York Times, February 28, 1986.

Saudi Arabian Oil Policy and the Iran-Iraq War

reaction to the successful Iranian offensive in February was to increase its oil production even more in an effort to stop Iran:

> Given the Ayatollah's fanaticism, strategic thinkers around the Gulf believe that Iran will be persuaded to stop fighting only when it is stone broke, unable to import either food or munitions.[143]

It was only in August, when the combination of American arms sales, which the Saudis knew about, and strong Iranian resistance to the price war, encouraged Saudi Arabia to back down somewhat, but not completely.

Though Iran came away from the August meeting the proclaimed power broke of OPEC, the actual agreement was a compromise that was not far from what Saudi Arabia had offered at the previous OPEC meeting in Yugoslavia. Iran did not get nearly as drastic a cut in OPEC production as it had hoped, and thee was little suggestion of an eventual price increase up to the $28 level which Iran had previously insisted on. Of even greater importance was the clause which allowed Iraq to be left out of the quota system. This concession was an open admission of Iran's financial desperation, and reflects a high degree of Iranian concessions. The final agreement called for an OPEC ceiling of 16.8 mbd for a two month test period after which delegates would return to decide upon a more permanent approach.[144]

There seemed to have been a virtually unanimous opinion that oil prices had simply sunk too low; as stated by Iran's oil minister Gholam Reza Agazadeh:

---

143 Milton Viorst, "Bankrupting the Ayatollah," New York Times, August 5, 1986.
144 Wall Street Journal, August 6, 1986.

Saudi Arabian Oil Policy and the Iran-Iraq War

> We all felt the price-war strategy was taking oil prices toward $5 (a barrel), which is simply unbelievable. That became the single element pulling us together on this agreement.[145]

Sheikh Zaki Yamani, the most outspoken proponent of the price war, agreed suggesting that economics had indeed played a role in cementing the agreement, but as Kuwait's oil minister, Khalifa al-Sabah declared, Kuwait "would abrogate the new agreement and increase its crude-oil sales once again if any OPEC member 'exceeded its quota by a single barrel.'"[146]

Therefore, although the August meeting must be viewed as a political victory for Iran and a defeat for Saudi Arabia, it was only a limited victory and did not drastically improve Iran's position in regards to revenue needs. An erosion of Saudi confidence in Iraq after Fao and Mehran, combined with the United States arms sales to Iran, forced Saudi Arabia to reconsider its price war, but did not yet mark a total reversal of Saudi policy.

In August, Iraq began a new series of attacks in the Gulf, especially on the newly developed terminal on Sirri Island, which had been built in response to Iraqi attacks on Kharg. On October 8, Iraq launched a particularly devastating attack against Kharg that virtually wiped out that facility's exports. By mid-October, Iranian production was down to about 600,000 barrels a day.[147]

At the OPEC meeting in October, armed with these successful Iraqi attacks, Saudi Arabia and Kuwait began pushing for a

---

145 ibid.
146 ibid.
147 New York Times, October 26, 1986.

greater percentage of the OPEC production quotas in an effort to block an agreement. Kuwait was particularly adamant that it should receive a 10% increase in its quota of 900,000 barrels a day.

> Some delegates accused the Saudis and Kuwaitis of staging the deadlock so that both countries would emerge as engineers of a major compromise. Iran, their political and economic rival, got credit for the current OPEC agreement, reached in August, which drove prices up from their summertime lows to their present levels of about $14.[148]

After sixteen days of bitter haggling (the longest OPEC meeting in history), a compromise was arranged that gave Kuwait a smaller immediate increase, but a greater increase in December. The meeting ended with the production limitations extended another month, and with Saudi Arabia backing down from its initial stance.

Iran at this point was in a very powerful position within OPEC, especially considering that the September OPEC production had actually come in below the agreed upon quota. The August agreement pressed by Iran seemed to have been a complete success. Only Saudi Arabia and Kuwait seemed to be opposing Iranian efforts within OPEC, and they had agreed to a continuation of the agreement for another month, backing down from their initial intention of blocking any further agreement.[149]

On October 30, 1986, Saudi Arabia announced that Sheikh Yamani had been removed from his position. There were

---
148 Wall Street Journal, October 22, 1986.
149 New York Times, October 14, 1986.

suggestions that Yamani was fired due to personal differences with King Fahd. These differences may or may not have existed, but still do not explain the reasons for firing Yamani. Rather than simply having him honorably replaced the papers announced the government's decision before Yamani was told of it. Yamani's removal as oil minister seemed to have a more political implication in that with his departure went "the last remnant of Saudi support for the price-war strategy," leaving Iran without opposition within OPEC.[150]

> Diplomats and oil industry sources say Sheik Ahmed Zaki Yamani was caught in (a) crossfire of increasingly strained Middle Eastern oil politics; his strategy of getting most long-term value out of nation's oil conflicted with increasing pressure on King Fahd from Iran, which wants higher income from oil.[151]

The December OPEC Agreement

By November, Iran had reached its height of influence within OPEC. Though Iraqi attacks upon Iranian oil installations were as sharp as ever, Iran's oft repeated threats of a final offensive seemed to be gaining in credibility. In early, November, it was disclosed that Iran had received large quantities of what at first was termed "spare parts" from the United States. This, combined with the circumstances of Yamani's dismissal, and a surprising ability of Iran to moderate and control OPEC, led to a solidifying of Iranian prestige and influence.

---

150 Wall Street Journal, October 30, 1986.
151 New York Times, October 31, 1986.

Saudi Arabian Oil Policy and the Iran-Iraq War

To do this, Iran successfully used a sophisticated carrot and stick approach with Saudi Arabia and the other Gulf states. Waving its next "final offensive" over the heads of the Arab states in OPEC, Iran at the same time offered concessions, both political and economic, for those who agreed to cooperate with its policies in OPEC:

> In the summer, Iran began talks with King Fahd, promising to back away from attacks on Saudi, Kuwait and other Arab-owned oil tankers in the Persian Gulf and to diminish its sponsorship of militant anti-Saudi elements in the Gulf region.[152]

In return, Iran got an end to the price war and a generally more cooperative Saudi Arabia. Saudi Arabia began selling to Iran large quantities of Saudi refined fuel, which Iran desperately needed for its war effort, and replaced Yamani with Hisham Nazer, a more conciliatory oil minister.[153]

At the December OPEC meeting in Geneva, Iran and Saudi Arabia worked in tandem to reach an accord that would raise OPEC's price up to around $18 a barrel. Production cuts were distributed evenly within OPEC with the goal of a 7% total reduction. The accord seemed tenable because of the tacit alliance between Iran and Saudi Arabia. As was reported, "the Saudi's acting minister, Hisham Nazer, worked closely with Iran's representative, Gholam Reza Agazadeh, to bring about the accord."[154] Only Iraq refused to go along with the proposal forcing Saudi Arabia to bring intense pressure against Iraq.

---

152 Wall Street Journal, December 22, 1986.
153 New York Times, November 23, 1986.
154 Wall Street Journal, December 22, 1986.

Saudi Arabian Oil Policy and the Iran-Iraq War

The Saudis did this by discovering "technical problems" in the Petroline pipeline, shared by both Iraq and Saudi Arabia, which could have carried some 500,000 barrels of a day of Iraqi oil to the Red Sea port of Yanbu:

> Saudi Arabia had closed down the shared pipeline. To expand it, but the work has been finished, and informed sources suggest that the delay in its reopening is a 'political decision.'[155]

The Saudi cooperation with the Iranians from August 1986 onward can be viewed as similar to the previous reversals of Saudi policies of price moderation in 1979 and in 1982. The difference here being that the level of Saudi economic loss was less severe in 1986 than in the earlier cases. The common thread that connects the three incidents is the fact that in all three cases, Saudi Arabia abandoned policies more in its favor due to radical political pressure in the Middle East and in OPEC. This is obvious when one considers the disastrous consequences of an Iranian victory, and the significance of Saudi Arabia's cooperation with Iran, giving Iran sorely needed revenue.

In 1986, Saudi Arabia had succeeded in virtually all its economic goals involved in the price war, but was forced to concede many points of political importance to Iran. This was due in large measure to the Reagan administrations decision to use weapons sales as negotiating tools with Iran, and apprehensions over Iraq's military performance. Saudi Arabia's appeasement of Iran in 1986 was possibly more significant than previous instances because in this case Saudi Arabia's actions may have provided important aid to the Iranians in their war against Iraq. Before, Saudi actions were simple reactions to uncontrollable situations, but in 1986,

---
155 ibid.

Saudi Arabian Oil Policy and the Iran-Iraq War

Saudi appeasement was a profoundly deep-seated policy decision on the part of the Saudi government. Its significance is tremendous considering the potential disaster an Iranian victory would hold for Saudi Arabia and the other Gulf conservatives, and how very defenseless they would be in such an event.

Chapter 7: Conclusion

The Noble Oil

> The official government view in Saudi Arabia may be described as the 'noble oil argument.' In other words, oil is too precious to burn as a fuel and therefore oil substitutes in the energy field should be developed as soon as possible... However, it is not being too cynical to ask the question as to whether the Saudis would really wish to see world importance of oil diminish, and with it their role in that world. Without the importance of oil, on the basis of population, Saudi Arabia would rank in the world power league along with Rwanda and Upper Volta. Thus Saudi Arabia is keen to price in such a way that the substitution effect is not too drastic.[156]

The most important thing that the student of Saudi Arabian oil policy must remember is that although oil is the sole factor in Saudi Arabia's importance as a nation, oil is not an end in itself. In providing revenue to the Saudi government, oil serves its first and most important function. As with all nations, Saudi Arabia has a variety of needs and goals, and its oil wealth has helped it progress towards these goals. The wealth that Saudi Arabia receives from oil sales allows it to advance its domestic welfare and its foreign influence. Yet

---
156 El-Mokadem, p. 50.

even with this, oil still serves a higher purpose: comprehensive Saudi political goals.

In the best of times, Saudi Arabian oil policy remains a tool, and in the worst of times it becomes a trap. The same wealth that lifted the Arabian peninsula out of the dark ages and into the twentieth century, has given Saudi Arabia political influence around the world. But at different times it has placed Saudi Arabia under great political pressure. For Saudi Arabia, the best of all possible worlds would be one in which it could produce its oil according to its financial needs and considerations, and in which political goals and economic goals could go hand in hand. At times Saudi Arabia has come close to realizing this ideal, but at other times Saudi Arabia has found its political interests and its economic interests in conflict. In such situations, Saudi Arabia has invariably chosen to follow its political interests even though they may have been detrimental to its economic interests.

In 1973, Saudi Arabia freely chose to abandon what it had previously espoused as economic rationality for a course of action that it felt was politically necessary. By supporting the embargo in 1973, though it proved economically damaging to the West, Saudi Arabia obtained five years of regional stability. Saudi actions kept Sadat from falling, and further secured the invaluable Egyptian-Saudi alliance. If not for the fall of the Shah, the regional balance of power created after 1973 could have lead to a more permanent solution to the Middle East question.

After 1973 however, Saudi Arabia experienced three more reversals of its economic policy which were the results of general Saudi political reversals. In 1973, Saudi Arabia acted on its own initiative, but in 1979, 1982, and 1986, Saudi Arabian policies were reactions to political coercion.

Saudi Arabian Oil Policy and the Iran-Iraq War

If in fact Saudi Arabian oil policy is but a part, albeit an important part, of the broader Saudi Arabian political agenda, then it becomes apparent that to accurately understand Saudi Arabian oil policy, one must put priority upon political issues above economics. By developing an understanding of the forces that play the most important role in Saudi oil policy, one can conceptualize a general direction in which it may be heading. In a politically stable environment, one can expect that rational oil policy will be a high priority for Saudi Arabian planners, but in a capricious political environment such as that which exists now in the Middle East, other issues will surely supersede oil policy in importance.

For Saudi Arabia, the period since the Iranian Revolution has been fraught with dangers and uncertainties. The Iran-Iraq War threatens to destabilize the entire Middle East, especially the oil rich Persian Gulf states. An Iranian victory would be a disaster for all its weaker neighbors, but even continued stalemate has the potential to further exacerbate the delicate balance of power within the Gulf. In such an environment, stable oil prices would seem to be purely a matter of chance, more than due to an easily discernible pattern of economic necessity.

In such an environment, it is difficult to place an upper ceiling and a lower floor on where oil prices could go to. Considering the profound oil glut, not just in short-term supplies, but in long-term reserves, there seems to be little likelihood of another price explosion any time soon. All the pressure seems to be for a downward trend in prices due to the vast quantities of oil which lies outside of OPEC. Efforts to just hold up the market under such conditions will require iron discipline from a powerful authority. At the moment, Iran and Saudi Arabia seem to be providing such leadership for OPEC, in a marriage of necessity that rests on Iran's dominance in the Gulf.

Saudi Arabian Oil Policy and the Iran-Iraq War

The next political upheaval could bring a tumble in the market rather than a price increase, but this all depends upon numerous factors within OPEC, and on the reactions of the West. If Iran wins the Iran-Iraq War, Saudi oil policy would be hostage to Iranian demands. Right now, the Iraqi army is the only real line of defense in place against Iran, and Iraq's situation seems tenuous at best. Saudi Arabia's hopes rest on Iraq being able to hold out against Iran, but outside of financial aid, Saudi Arabia does not seem able to give sufficient and unqualified support to Iraq. Saudi Arabia's future depends upon the outcome of the Iran-Iraq War, but as with all things in the Middle East, there can be no certainty.

Saudi Arabian Oil Policy and the Iran-Iraq War

Post Script

The analysis contained herein goes up to the end of 1986. At that point in the Iran-Iraq War, Iran looked to be winning. However, after several more Iraqi defeats in 1987, the Iraqi high command convinced Saddam Hussein to give them more freedom to fight the war without his constant personal interference. Saddam Hussein agreed, and the entire country was placed on a defensive war footing.

The results were surprising. Iraq began to turn the war around, and by the summer of 1988 most of the Iranian successes were reversed. Iraq utilized every weapon at their disposal, including chemical weapons. Without interference from Saddam Hussein, Iraq was able to launch well coordinated and successful offensives against Iran, and Iran found that their human wave attacks were ineffective. By the end of the summer of 1988, Iraq had capture most of Iran's heavy equipment such as tanks and artillery, and Iran lacked the funds to be able to replace the losses.

In the Fall of 1988 the Iranians accepted UN backed peace negotiations and the war ended with Iraq holding a clear advantage over Iran.

At the beginning of 1989, the Iraqi military seemed to be supreme in the Middle East. It was certainly superior to that of the Saudis and the other Gulf states. Iraq began making demands from his neighbors and from OPEC, and accusing Kuwait of stealing Iraqi oil.

Saudi Arabian Oil Policy and the Iran-Iraq War

In August of 1990, Saddam Hussein was confident enough to launch an invasion of Kuwait overrunning the small country in a few days. Some suggest his confidence was based upon poor communications from US diplomatic officials leading the Iraqis to believe the USA would not oppose such an invasion.

This turned out to be in error. The USA led an international coalition of nations that not only liberated Kuwait from Iraqi control, but also effectively destroyed the Iraqi military as an offensive force.

BIBLIOGRAPHY

Allen, Loring. OPEC Oil. Cambridge, Massachusetts: Delgeshlager, Gunn, and Hain, Publ. Inc., 1979.

Badger, Daniel and Robert Belgrave. Oil Supply and Price: What Went Right in 1980? London: Royal Institute of International Affairs, 1982.

Doran, Charles F. "OPEC Structure and Cohesion: Exploring the Determinant of Cartel Policy." Journal of Politics, (February 1980).

El-Mallack, Rageai, ed. OPEC: Twenty Years and Beyond. Boulder, Colorado: Westview Press, 1982.

El-Mokadem. OPEC and the World Oil Market 1973-1983. London: Easlords Publishing Ltd, 1984.

Gately, Dermot. "A Ten-Year Retrospective: OPEC and the World Oil Market." Journal of Economic Literature, (September 1984), pp. 1100-1114.

Gilpin, Kenneth N. "Saudi Economy is Ailing." New York Times. (February 18, 1985), Section D, p. 31.

Golub, David G. When Oil and Politics Mix: Saudi Oil Policy. 1973-1985. Cambridge, Massachusetts: Center For Middle Eastern Studies, Harvard University, 1985.

Griffin, James M. and David J. Teece, ed. OPEC Behavior and World Oil Prices. Boston: George Allen, & Unwin, 1982.

Hershey, Robert D. "Accord Called Evidence of Limit to Saudi Power." New York Times, (March 15, 1983), Section D, p.22.

Ibrahim, Youssef M. "Iran-Iraq War a Set Back to Saudi Role in OPEC." New York Times, (October 16,1980), Section D, p. 1.

Jaidah, Ali M. An Appraisal of OPEC Oil Policies. New York: Longman, 1983.

Kanovsky, Eliyahu. "On Saudi Oil Policy." New York Times, (December 19, 1980), p. 35.

----------. Saudi Arabia's Dismal Economic Future: Regional and Global Implications. Occasional Papers. Tel Aviv, Israel: The Dayan Center for Middle Eastern and African Studies, The Shiloah Institute, April 1986.

----------. "The Rise and Fall of Arab Oil Power," Chemtech, (November 1986), p. 65.

Koopman, Georg and Klaus Matthies, Beate Reszat. Oil and the International Economy. Hamburg: Hamburg Institute of Economic Research, 1984.

Lacey, Robert. The Kingdom: Arabia and the House of Sa'ud. New York: Avon Books, 1981.

Levy, Walter. Oil Strategy and Politics. Boulder, Colorado: Westview Press, 1982.

Moran, Theodore H. "Modeling OPEC Behavior: Economic and Political Alternatives." International Organization, (Spring 1981), pp. 241-272.

----------. Oil Prices and the Future of OPEC. Washington, D.C.: Resources for the Future, 1978.

Mylroie, Laurie Ann. Regional Security After Empire: Saudi and the Gulf. PhD thesis, Harvard University, 1985.

Noreng, Oystein. Oil Politics in the 1980s. New York: 1980s Project/Council on Foreign Relations, McGraw-Hill Book Co.

Odell, Peter R. Oil and World Power. seventh ed. New York: Penguin Books, 1983.

Quandt, William B. Saudi Arabia in the 1980s: Foreign Policy. Security. and Oil. Washington, D.C.: The Brookings Institute, 1981.

----------. Saudi Arabia's Oil Policy, Washington, D.C.: The Brookings Institute, 1981.

Pearce, Joan, ed. The Third Oil Shock: The Effects of Lower Prices. London: The Royal Institute of International Affairs, 1982.

Pearson, John, Ed. "The Saudies Had to Pump More Oil or Lose Mideast Influence." Business Week, (December 30, 1985), p.65.

Pindyck, Robert S. "OPEC's Threat to the West." Foreign Policy. (Spring 1978b, 30), pp. 36-52.

Rowen, Henry S. "Saudi Gambit Can Succeed," Wall Street Journal, (March 21, 1986).

Safran, Nadav. Saudi Arabia: The Ceaseless Quest for Security. Cambridge, Massachusetts: The Belknap Press of Harvard University Press, 1985.

Sampson, Anthony. The Seven Sisters. New York: Bantam Books, 1975.

Sterner, Michael. "The Iran-Iraq War." Foreign Affairs.(Fall 1984).

Vicker, Ray. The Kingdom of Oil: The Middle East; Its People and its Power. New York: Charles Scribner's Sons, 1974.

Viorst, Milton. "Bankrupting the Ayatollah," New York Times. (August 5, 1986), Sect. I. p. 23.

Journals and Annuals

Business Week. (U.S.)

British Petroleum Statistical Review of World Energy 1982. (U.K.)

The Middle East. Abstract and Index. (Egypt)

The Middle East Contemporary Survey. (Tel Aviv)

The Middle East Economic Digest. (U.K.)

Monthly Energy Review. (U.S.)

Monthly Bulletin of Statistics. (U.N.)

New York Times. (U.S.)

Petroleum Intelligence Weekly. (U.S.)

Wall Street Journal. (U.S.)

About the Author

Alexander John Hay graduated from Harvard University with an AB in Political Science Cum Laude in 1987. From 1987 to 1988, he was a Fulbright Scholar studying Arabic and traveling in the Middle East. He briefly worked in the petrochemical construction industry prior to entering law school. He graduated from the University of Houston Law Center in May of 1992, and became licensed to practice law in the State of Texas on November 6, 1992. Alexander John Hay is currently practicing law as a sole proprietor.

For more information visit: **www.Alexander-Hay.com** or email your questions or comments to **ahay@alexander-hay.com**

www.ingramcontent.com/pod-product-compliance
Lightning Source LLC
Chambersburg PA
CBHW031432210526
45464CB00005B/2169